Guide to SILVERMARKS of the World

Guide to SILVERMARKS of the World

Jan Diviš

TIGER BOOKS INTERNATIONAL

Designed and produced by
Aventinum Publishers, Prague, Czech Republic
Text by Jan Diviš
Translated by Joy Moss-Kohoutová
Marks drawings by Jaromír Knotek
Graphic design by Aleš Krejča

This edition published in 1998 by
Tiger Books International PLC,
Twickenham, UK

ISBN 1-84056-085-1
Printed in the Czech Republic
by Polygrafia, a.s., Prague
2/10/16/51-01

CONTENTS

INTRODUCTION

Hallmarks stamped on silver items are intended to protect the buyer. They guarantee that the content of the precious metal in every individual piece corresponds to legal requirements. However, for us today the hallmarks on antique silver pieces are also invaluable aids in determining the place and date they were produced, which is the most important and most necessary information. This book is intended as a guide to the most important of these marks and a practical and ready source of information to the amateur and specialist alike — in fact to everyone who, for love of it or in the line of duty, comes into contact with "the Queen of Metals".

This handbook has therefore been compiled according to these practical considerations and starts from what the observer sees: the arrangement of the marks — based on the subjects they depict — enables the reader speedily and easily to make his way around in the book, and the text concerning the drawings of the individual marks tells him about the town and country where the hallmark was used, the date when it was employed and, if possible, the purity which the mark guarantees. The marks are arranged according to the following pattern: letters in alphabetical order (1—669), numerals (670—695), human figures (696—887), mammals (888—1140), birds (1141—1302), other animals (1303—1359), plants (1360—1482), heavenly bodies (1483—1517), architecture (1518—1591), objects (1592—1816), emblems (1817—1994).

Regarding the origin and age of the items, the most reliable answer is provided by marks stamped by control bodies, whether these were municipalities, state institutions or guilds. These marks have been incorporated in this book to the fullest extent of present-day knowledge. Furthermore, those marks which are unusually important in determining the country and place of origin of the item have been included, such as a special duty mark, or the assignee's hallmark. The other hallmarks (maker's marks, date letters, special marks for purity, etc.) had to be omitted because they would have gone beyond the bounds of this volume. However, an elementary choice of marks of silversmiths working in the U.S.A. has been included because in the United States there was no state or other control of purity standards and so the hallmarks of American producers are the only indication determining items of American provenance.

The origin and development of marking differed in individual countries and states of the world. This is explained in the brief outline of marking and hallmark regulations which follows, presented by countries and states whose marks are included in this book and whose silver products deserve attention. If the name of a goldsmith appears in the book it should be remembered that in most countries the goldsmith made items of both gold and silver; a goldsmith was anyone who worked with precious metals, and, in most cases, not even official decrees distinguished between a goldsmith and a silversmith.

It is hoped that this book will be of help chiefly to lovers of antique silver and, therefore, the main stress is on hallmarks used in the past. For this reason the most recent date for the choice of marks is the period between the world wars, i.e. the 1930s.

Prague, November 1974 Jan Diviš

HALLMARKING IN INDIVIDUAL STATES

AUSTRALIA

No official marks exist in Australia for items made of precious metals since most of the silver pieces are imported from England.

In 1923 producers attempted to introduce marks for several Australian areas. These marks, however, provided no official guarantees and are no longer used.

AUSTRIA

1366 — a decree of the Austrian Princes Albrecht and Leopold was issued on assaying precious metals. Two guild masters were named to test the purity, both being under the supervision of the master of the mint.

1659 — a patent of Emperor Leopold I permitted work in 14 lot silver.

1708 — a patent of Emperor Joseph I permitted a purity of 13 lots and 14 lots (known as the Augsburger und Wiener-Probe).

1737 — a patent of Emperor Charles VI introduced a purity standard of 15 lots.

1774 — a patent of Empress Maria Theresa depicted for the first time the hallmarks that had to be used.

1784 — beginning with this year, state control of purity commenced in Austria — but only in Vienna.

1786 — state control of purity was introduced in Galicia (see Poland).

1806 — a uniform state system of marking throughout the entire Austro-Hungarian Empire was introduced, except for Hungary, Slovakia (under Hungarian domination), and Transylvania.

1866 — from 1 August new hallmarks and marks of purity for silver, calculated in thousandths instead of the previous lot system, became valid. These hallmarks are now used in Hungary as well. Permitted purity standards are 950, 900, 800 and 750/1000.

1872 — the marks in use were altered so that the letter indicating the seat of the assay office became part of the purity mark. These marks were used in the Austrian Republic until 1921, in Czechoslovakia until 1922, in part of Poland until 1920, in part of Yugoslavia until 1919, and in Hungary until 1937.

1921 — marks of the new Austrian Republic came into force with the law of 21 October.

Bibliography:

Knies, K.: Die Punzirung in Österreich. Vienna 1896.

Reitzner, V.: Alt-Wien-Lexikon für Österreichische u. Süddeutsche Kunst u. Kunstgewerbe. Band III.: Edelmetalle u. deren Punzen. Vienna 1952.

BELGIUM

1484 — Maximilian issued a decree for his Flanders territories evidently affecting the use of date letters.

1501 — Archduke Philip the Handsome, as Governor of the Netherlands, issued regulations for goldsmiths in Holland, Seeland, and Friesland and on 2 February, 1502, for Antwerp, and probably for other towns as well.
Hallmarked items: 1. town emblem under the crown; 2. date letter; 3. maker's mark.

1551 — in Brussels Emperor Charles V issued goldsmiths' regulations for the Netherlands which also applied to part of northern France (Artois), today's Belgium (except for the principality of Liège), the Grand Duchy of Luxemburg and the Kingdom of the Netherlands.

1556 — the Netherlands came under the Spanish line of the Habsburgs. The existing system of hallmarking remained in force.

1612 — Governor Albrecht issued a decree ordering the introduction of another hallmark, in addition to the town mark already in use.
A specimen of hallmarking from this time:

a, b) Ypres town marks; c) date letter 1684/85; d) maker's mark (P. Vost).

1797 — Austria's Netherlands came under French rule. French rulings of 1797 (19th Brumaire Year VI) now became valid.

1815—30 — Belgium formed part of the Kingdom of the Netherlands, but marks other than those used in the Netherlands were used on Belgian territory.

1831 — following the establishment of the Kingdom of Belgium a new ruling was issued on hallmarking, based on the French model. Hallmarking became obligatory.

1869 — the law of 5 June, 1868, came into force, abolishing obligatory state control and permitting any standard of purity. Nevertheless, items with a purity of 800 and 900/1000 could be submitted for assaying and marked. State marks of purity were introduced as well as the personal marks of the assayers. The maker's mark was not required. These marks remained in force until 1 January, 1942.

Bibliography:

Crooÿ L. and F.: Les Poinçons Belges d'Orfèvrerie depuis le XVe s. jusqu à la Révolution Française. Brussels 1910.

BULGARIA

Nothing is known about the hallmarking of items made of precious metals in Bulgaria in older times. This is evidently the result of the Turkish occupation which lasted from 1393 to 1878 (and in the south of the country until 1881). Hallmarking was probably carried out according to the Turkish system.

1910 — the law of 1 March, 1907, came into force. Items were marked with an official stamp of purity and the maker's mark. Permitted fineness standards were 950, 900, 850, 750 and 500/1000.

Bibliography:

Georgieva, S. — Buchinski, D.: Staroto zlatarstvo v Vratsa. Sofia 1959.

Zontshev, J.: Der Goldschatz von Panagjurischste. 1950.

CANADA

Silversmiths who settled in Canada in the period when it was a French colony (1700—1763) used marks similar to those of French makers: the first letters of the maker's name shown in a shield and over them either a crown or the French fleur de lis or else a star. After 1763, during the period of British rule, the marks of Canadian makers changed. Only the monogram of the maker remained in the shield which was now rectangular or semi-circular. These hallmarks are very similar to the marks of goldsmiths from the Channel Islands and therefore, when it comes to identification, mistakes can easily be made. Goldsmiths in the provinces of Montreal and Quebec added the word MONTREAL or QUEBEC to their marks at this time. The goldsmiths from Halifax (Nova Scotia) similarly added the monogram "H" or "HX", or "XNS". The monograms "StJ" or "NB" were used in St John (New Brunswick). At the beginning of the 19th century Canadian hallmarks imitated English ones.

Examples even occur of imitations of the English official hallmarks, for instance the duty mark. In 1908 a law came into effect — valid until 1946 — requiring a purity of 925/1000 in silver work.

Bibliography:

Langdon, J. E.: Canadian Silversmiths and their Marks. Vermont 1960.

CZECHOSLOVAKIA

1324 — the oldest record of a goldsmiths' brotherhood in Prague.

1562 — Ferdinand I approved the guild rules of Prague goldsmiths. All items weighing more than half a hřivna (a Prague hřivna weighed c. 253 grams; 64 Prague groschen were made from one hřivna) had to be submitted to the guild for testing. The items had to be marked as follows: 1. town mark; 2. maker's mark (mostly monogram).

1776 — new guild regulations for Prague goldsmiths. Provision for the election of three makers to hallmark silver pieces. The Prague goldsmith's guild was the so-called Land Guild, i.e. all goldsmiths in the Kingdom of Bohemia were obliged to observe its regulations. Only 13 lot silver was permitted to be used. A special hallmark was decreed for lower standards of purity.

1785 — 15 lot silver was allowed to be used and a new mark was introduced for it.

1788 — the following purities for silver were stipulated by law: 13 lot (= 812.5/1000) and 15 lot (= 937.5/1000). Hallmarking was still carried out by appointed guild masters. Now, items were marked with three stamps: 1. the maker's mark; 2. the mark of Bohemia (for Prague), or the mark of the town where the maker worked; 3. the mark of purity.

1806 — a basic change occurred in the hereditary Austrian lands in hallmarking precious metals: the right to mark the products was taken from the guilds and given to the state. (For details on this and subsequent changes see Austria.)

1921 — old Austrian marks of 1872 were abolished and Czechoslovak hallmarks were introduced. Permitted purity: 950, 900, 800 and 750/1000.

1929 — introduction of new marks and new purities of 959, 925, 900, 835 and 800/1000. These marks were valid until 1940.

Note: Slovakia, as part of the former Austro-Hungarian Empire, belonged to Hungary until 1918 and was naturally subject to Hungarian regulations.

Bibliography:

Hráský, J.: Značkování výrobků z drahých kovů (In: Pražský sborník historický VIII), Prague 1973.

Schirek, C.: Die Punzierung in Mähren. Brno 1902.

DENMARK

1445 — a royal decree, valid throughout the kingdom, required that every item be stamped with a town hallmark and a maker's mark.

1523 — until this year, Danish regulations were generally valid for Sweden.

1685 — a decree was issued by Christian IV for Copenhagen, which was the model for other towns of the kingdom as well as for larger towns of Norway, introduced basic changes in the system of marking: each object weighing over 5 lots had to be submitted to the master of the mint for assay. The master then marked it with the town emblem, with a mark of the month, and with his own mark. Henceforth there were four marks on an item: 1. the town mark (København); 2. the assayer's mark (master C. Ludolf); 3. the mark of the month (April); 4. the maker's mark.

1814 — until this year Danish regulations applied to Norway as well.

1893 — the law of 5 April, 1888, came into force. Items had now to be marked with 1. the producer's mark; 2. the purity figure with the letter "S"; 3. an official mark with date. The lowest permissible purity standard was 826/1000.

Bibliography:

Boje, Ch. A.: Danske Guld og Solf Smedemaeker for 1870. Copenhagen 1951.

Orlik, J.: Danske Guldsmedes Maerker. Copenhagen 1919.

EGYPT

From 1 September, 1916, the hallmarking system established by the law of 8 August, 1906, came into force. Items produced in Egypt were stamped with three marks:

1. purity and assay office (Cairo 800/1000); 2. government mark; 3. date letter.

These three marks were stamped on all the main parts of a product. Small items were only marked with a stamp of quality. The law of 1906 and the marks used were valid until 1946.

ENGLAND

First records of English goldsmiths' guilds date from the 12th century.

1180 — Henry II; establishment of a goldsmiths' guild having the right to use the hallmark with the leopard's head.

1238 — Henry III; introduction of a silver purity assay to avoid fraud.

1300—1544 — Edward I; in this period the hallmark with the leopard's head indicated the Sterling standard of purity of 11 oz 2 dwt (= 925/1000), corresponding to the purity of the coinage instituted in the reign of Henry II (1154—89).

1336 — the goldsmiths' guild issued regulations on hallmarking and introduced the following marks:
1. leopard's head;
2. maker's mark;
3. date letter.

Leopard's head, the hallmark for London, was also used by Exeter and York from the 18th century.

Maker's marks consisted first of symbols, then during the 17th century of letters (generally the initials of the maker's Christian name and surname or of the surnames of a partnership) either alone or with a symbol, a favourite one being a crown or coronet. During the period of the Britannia Standard (1697—1720), however, it was compulsory for the maker's mark to consist of the first two letters of his surname.

Date letter for London was changed every year in May and indicates the age of the piece. When the alphabet was exhausted (twenty letters from A to U were used, excluding J), the shape of the letter and shield was changed. Other towns with assay offices each had their own system.

1423 — introduction of the "mark of origin". Every office had its own mark, for instance London had the leopard's head.

The subsequent development of English hallmarking might seem very complicated, but the whole problem can be explained by using the example of the marking system employed in London (the specimen marks are based on M. Rosenberg).

Until 1544 silver items were stamped with three marks:
1. leopard's head;
2. date letter;
3. maker's mark.

Specimen:

MAKER'S MARK

In 1544 a fourth mark was added, the "lion passant". The model for this was taken from the royal emblem. It indicated the "Sterling" purity — 11 oz 2 dwt (= 925/1000). As the symbol of Sterling purity it was used in the other towns of England as well. Until 1821 the lion was shown en face, thereafter in profile.

Specimen:

MAKER'S MARK

From 1697 to 1720 the required purity was 11 oz 10 dwt (= 958.3/1000), with these hallmarks: a) figure of Britannia, b) lion's head erased, superseding and replacing marks 1 and 4 (leopard's head and lion passant).

Products of Britannia standard were stamped with four marks as follows: 1. figure of Britannia; 2. lion's head erased; 3. date letter; 4. maker's mark.

Specimen:

MAKER'S MARK

Since the silver "Britannia" purity proved too soft for general everyday use, in 1719 an Act was passed enabling silversmiths to return to the normal Sterling standard from 1 June, 1720, so that henceforth both series of hallmarks were used side by side. In 1784 for England and Scotland (but not for Ireland), a duty mark was introduced confirming that a tax had been paid for the purity assay. It showed the head of the ruling king or queen and was used until 1890. Therefore, from 1784 onwards every work of silver had five different marks:

1. leopard's head; 2. date letter; 3. lion passant;
4. duty mark; 5. maker's mark.

Specimen:

MAKER'S MARK

From 1890, once again four marks were in use, since the duty mark was abolished:

A/ For lower purity:
1. leopard's head; 2. date letter; 3. lion passant;
4. maker's mark.

Specimen:

MAKER'S MARK

B/ For higher purity:
1. date letter; 2. Britannia; 3. lion's head erased;
4. maker's mark.

Specimen:

MAKER'S MARK

Bibliography:

Bradbury, F.: British and Irish Silver Assay Office Marks 1544—1954. London 1955.

Jackson, C. J.: English Goldsmiths and their Marks. London 1949.

Taylor, G.: Silver. Harmondsworth 1956.

Watts, W. W.: Old English Plate. 1924.

FINLAND

14th century — Finland was occupied by Sweden.

1743 — part of the country was occupied by Russia.

1809 — the whole country was occupied by Russia. Until this year, Swedish hallmarking was valid on the territory of Finland.

1810 — henceforth, new hallmarking was introduced (different from the Russian system: 1. state mark with the Finnish crown; 2. date letter (A = 1810; A2 = 1864; A3 = 1888, etc). 3. mark of purity in lots or zolotniks (13 L = 78 zolotniks = 812.5/1000); 4. maker's mark.

1920 — after liberalization, introduced in this year, the following purity became standard: 813 H = 830/1000; 916 H = 935/1000.

Bibliography:

Borg, Tyra: Guld och Silversmeder i Finland. Helsinki 1935.

FRANCE

1275 — a decree of Philip the Bold required the marking of silver objects with the town and maker's marks.

1577 — for fiscal reasons Henry III tried to introduce a new control hallmark (droit de remède).

1579 — Henry III; a new attempt to introduce another mark. Revenues from this mark were to be given to an assignee. The king's plan failed because of opposition by Parisian goldsmiths.

1672 — a new tax (droit de marque sur l'or et l'argent) was introduced. The collection of the tax was assigned and its payment was indicated on the object with a special mark.

1681 — another hallmark was added to the original single mark of the assignee. In practice hallmarking was carried out as follows (Rosenberg):

1. Before the maker completed the item, i. e. mainly before putting the parts together, he stamped each part of the object with his own mark, the so-called "poinçon à contre saign", later known as the "poinçon de maître".

2. The marked parts of the item were submitted in the "bureau de la régie" to the officials of an assignee who marked the product with a stamp known as "poinçon de charge". This mark indicated that the item was subject to taxation.

3. But the maker was not yet allowed to complete the item; he had now to submit it to the guild — "bureau de la maison commune" — where guild assayers (gardes des communautés) examined the fineness of the individual parts and stamped them with the town hallmark (usually also with the letter indicating the year), the so-called "poinçon de la maison commune".

4. The goldsmith could then complete the piece. Upon completion, however, and before selling it, he had to go to the "bureau de la régie" again where, after paying the assignee's fee, the item was stamped with the so-called "poinçon de décharge". Only then could the product be placed on sale. The object was therefore stamped with four marks. Since the hallmarks of the guild assayers and assignees changed according to the size of the object, according to the purity of the metal, according to the person of the assignee, and according to the revenue district (généralités), their number runs into thousands and to this day not all of them have been reliably ascertained.

1791 — the system of assignees was abolished and thus the "charge" and "décharge" marks disappeared.

1797 — a new system of hallmarking was introduced. The test of purity was taken over by the state. Henceforth purity was indicated by the "poinçon de titre", and payment of the revenue tax by the "poinçon de garantie".

Explanation of certain special terms:

Poinçon de reconnaissance — the hallmark of the assignees, introduced in 1750 to indicate newly added parts to an older object. Otherwise the name for various types of markings.

Poinçon de recense — new assignees could either retain the hallmarks of their predecessors, or have new ones made for them. In the event of a new hallmark being introduced, a general review was carried out in which objects that had been taxed by the predecessor of the new assignee were stamped with a special hallmark, free of charge. The first gratuituous review came about in 1722 when spurious assignee hallmarks were discovered.

Poinçon de vieux — a hallmark for older items which appeared for resale, but had been hallmarked earlier by an assignee.

Bibliography:

Boivin, J.: Les Anciens Orfèvres Français et leurs Poinçons. Paris 1923.

Carré, L.: Les Poinçons de l'Orfévrerie Française. Paris 1928.

Cripps, W. J.: Old French Plate. London 1893.

Nocq, H.: Les Poinçons de Paris. Paris 1926.

Tardy: Les Poinçons de garantie internationaux pour l'argent. Paris 1974.

GERMANY

1289 — first mention of hallmarking objects in Erfurt.

1548 — an imperial law was issued on the basis of which all objects weighing more than 4 lots and produced from 14 lot silver had to be submitted for assay and provided with the mark of the maker and that of the town, or possibly the nobleman on whose territory the goldsmith had settled.

1667 — the stipulations found in the imperial law of 1548 were repeated.

1888 — on 1 January uniform hallmarks were introduced throughout the territory of Germany. Since that time, objects were hallmarked as follows: 1. maker's mark; 2. purity in figures (in thousandths); 3. crescent mark with a crown (stamped by the maker himself if the silver is of higher purity than 800/1000).

Bibliography:

Rosenberg, M.: Der Goldschmiede Merkzeichen. Frankfurt a. M. 1922.

Scheffler, W.: Goldschmiede Niedersachsens. Berlin 1965.
Stierling, H.: Goldschmiedezeichen von Altona bis Tondern. Neumünster 1955.

GREECE

Regulations for controlling the purity of objects made of precious metals did not exist until the 1930s: that is, until the end of the period covered by this book. According to a police regulation, goldsmiths were obliged to register their names and their marks with the local authorities of the town and inform the police of the purchase and sale of precious metals.

HUNGARY

1500 — until 1500 hallmarking was not customary in Hungary. Some objects from the 14th and 15th centuries bear hallmarks but neither their significance, nor the system of hallmarking, has as yet been clarified.

1504 — the oldest regulation on hallmarking in Hungary was issued by Vladislav, the King of Bohemia, Poland and Hungary. The mark is called "signum communae czechae". It was stamped next to the maker's mark. From the name of the mark it is evident that the purity control was carried out by the guild. This system was valid on the territory of Hungary (and Slovakia, which until 1918 was part of Hungary) until 1866.

1866 — 1 August, a new system of hallmarking was introduced, valid for the whole territory of the former Austro-Hungarian Empire (see Austria). These marks were in force on Hungarian territory until 1937.

Bibliography:

Köszeghy, E.: Merkzeichen der Goldschmiede Ungarns vom Mittelalter bis 1867. Budapest 1936.

IRELAND

1495 — adoption of English regulations of 1423.
1498 — a goldsmiths' guild existed in Dublin.
1557 — the manufacture of precious metals was liberalized in Dublin.
1605 — the test of purity was renewed in Dublin because liberalization had been abused.
1637 — Charles I approved the statutes of the goldsmiths' guild in Dublin, valid for the whole of Ireland. It was decreed that the purity of silver must not be lower than the English standard.
1638 — introduction of date letters.
1729 — introduction of a "duty" tax from 25 March, 1730. Payment of the tax was confirmed on the object by stamping with the "Hibernia" marks.
1807 — Ireland adopted the English hallmarking system, following the Act of Union with England in 1800.
1923 — new marks were introduced from 4 April, 1923, after the restoration of independence. Henceforth, objects were marked as follows: 1. maker's mark; 2. town mark; 3. mark of purity; 4. date letter.

ITALY

The disintegration of the ancient Roman empire into small, free territories or towns prevented the introduction of a uniform system of hallmarking on the territory of present-day Italy until modern times. In towns, the guilds usually stamped their hallmarks; territorial states introduced their own hallmarking systems.
1797 — the Republic of Venice on whose territory there had been a uniform system of hallmarking, organized by the state, came to an end. In addition to the city of Venice, this territory included Verona, Brescia, Bergamo and Friuli, part of Istria and nearly the whole of Dalmatia.
1810 — a decree by Napoleon introduced into the Kingdom of Italy a hallmarking system based on

the French model, with guarantee offices in Milan, Venice, Ancona, Verona and Brescia.

1815—59 (1866) — the French system remained in force on the territory occupied by Austria (Kingdom of Lombardy-Venice). Hallmarking offices were set up in Milan and Venice.

1818—72 — a special system of hallmarking was valid in the principalities of Modena and Parma during this period.

1873 — according to the law of 2 May, 1872, uniform hallmarking for the whole of Italy became valid. Manufacture was liberalized, the control of purity was not obligatory. Purities of 950, 900 and 800/1000 were introduced.

1935 — introduction of new marks and purities of 925 and 800/1000 valid to this day.

Bibliography:

Bulgari, C. G.: Argentieri, gemmari e orfi d'Italia. Roma 1958—69.

Sidney, J. A. — Churchill: The Goldsmiths of Italy. London 1926.

JAPAN

In Japan the hallmarking of objects made of precious metals was introduced in 1928 by the ministerial decree No 12 of 29 June. It was revised on 18 May, 1954. The permitted purity is given in thousandths in the following values: 1000, 950, 925, 900 and 800/1000. Silver objects must be marked according to the following specimen:

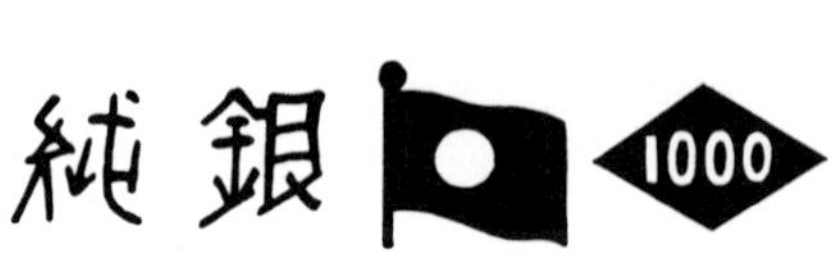

1. maker's mark; 2. control mark; 3. hallmark showing fineness.

NETHERLANDS

Until the wars of liberation against the Spaniards, the regulations applying to Spanish provinces were in force on the territory of the present-day Netherlands.

1501 — Archduke Philip issued goldsmiths' regulations for Holland, Seeland and Friesland (see Belgium).

1661 — the "Placaat en Ordonnante" was issued introducing the function of sworn assayers. These added to the maker's mark the town mark (merk van Stads Wapen) and a hallmark with the crowned lion (Provincialen gekroonden Leeuw), which guaranteed a higher content of precious metal (875/1000). Thus, on big pieces four marks were stamped according to this specimen:

1. town mark (Amsterdam); 2. date letter (in this instance 1608); 3. crowned lion; 4. maker's mark. For smaller items the maker's mark and the hallmark with the lion were required.

1806—10 — Kingdom of the Netherlands: new hallmarks for purities of 934 and 833/1000 and new date letters were established.

1810—14 — The Netherlands were joined to France.

1811 — the French system of hallmarking was introduced on the Emperor's orders. The items were marked with 1. the maker's mark; 2. a mark of purity; 3. the mark "bureau de garantie" (see France).

1814 — a royal decree established new marks valid only on the territory of the present-day Netherlands. On the territory of present-day Belgium, which until 1830 was part of the Netherlands, other hallmarks were used. Marks from 1814 were valid until 1953.

Bibliography:

Voet, E. Jr. and P. W. Voet: Nederlandse Goud- en Zilvermerken 1445—1951. The Hague 1951.

Voet, E.: Nederlandse Goud- en Zilversmeden, 1445—1951. The Hague 1963.

NORWAY

1314 — King Haakon V of Norway issued a decree requiring silver to be stamped with a purity mark.

1380—1814 — the union of Norway and Denmark — Danish regulations were in force.

1568 — a goldsmiths' guild was founded in Bergen.

1640—1740 — guilds were abolished and goldsmiths were directly subordinated to the king.

1740—1840 — the guilds were allowed again but their powers were very much curtailed.

1740 — henceforth hallmarks appeared for the individual months, first in the form of a fraction.

1766—1820 — hallmarks for the individual months depicted the signs of the zodiac.

A specimen of hallmarking from this period:

1. town mark (Bergen); 2. maker's mark (P. A. Aasmundsen); 3. mark of the year (1812); 4. assayer's mark (M. Pettersen); 5. mark of the month.

1859 — the guilds were once more abolished.

1891 — the law of 6 June introduced a modern system of hallmarking. The hallmark must have the purity in thousandths, the letter "S" next to the mark of purity, and the name of the maker. The lowest permitted purity is 830/1000.

Specimen:

830 S

---

name of the maker

The hallmark of officially assayed purity is the Norwegian lion with a crown.
The assay is optional.

Bibliography:

Vestlandske Kunstindustrimuseums Aarborg for Aaret 1903. Bergen 1903.

Krohn, H. T.: Trondhejms Gullsmedkunst 1550—1850. Oslo 1963.

POLAND

1548 — town marks are said to have been introduced by Sigismund August. Evidently a uniform hallmarking system was not yet in force. The hallmarking systems and marks changed with the different regimes in the territory of Poland:

1772 — the First Partition of Poland. Prussia occupied Polish Pomerania and western Prussia (except for Gdansk and Torun) and part of Great Poland. Austria seized Galicia (without Cracow), and Russia the territory at the Upper Dvina and the Dnieper.

1793 — the Second Partition of Poland. Prussia took Gdansk, Torun, most of Great Poland, Kujawy and Mazowsze, Russia the rest of White Russia, Podolye, Volhynia and the Ukraine.

1795 — the Third Partition of Poland. Russia seized the territory as far as the Bug and Niemen rivers, Prussia the rest of Great Poland with Warsaw, and Austria the whole of Little Poland with Cracow. Poland as an independent state ceased to exist.

1815—63 — following Napoleon's defeat, a new Polish Kingdom was created, ruled by the Russian Tsar. Galicia continued to remain under

Austrian administration, just as Prussia retained most of the territory it had seized earlier. Cracow and environs were declared a free republic.

1846 — Cracow was occupied by Austria. Until 1918 it remained part of the Austro-Hungarian Empire.

1863 — following the Warsaw Rising, the special privileges of the Polish Kingdom were abolished and it was then administered as the Russian Vistula Territory.

1920 — after the re-establishment of Poland, new hallmarks were introduced on 9 August. Permitted purities were 940, 875, 800/1000. These marks were valid until 1947.

Bibliography:

Bujańska, J.: Stare Srebra. Cracow 1972.

Lepszy, L.: Przemysł złotniczy w Polsce. Cracow 1933.

Myszkówna, H.: Srebra Warszawskie XVIII i XIX wieku w zbiorach Muzeum Historycznego. Warsaw 1973.

PORTUGAL

Before the introduction of a state hallmarking system in 1881, the individual towns had their own marks. The maker's mark was also required. Town marks guaranteed a purity of 958/1000.

1881 — introduction of a provisional state hallmarking system.

1886 — introduction of obligatory control of purity by a decree of 1 June. Permitted purity 916 and 833/1000.

1938 — 1 January introduction of new marks valid to this day. The system of hallmarking has remained the same.

Bibliography:

Dos Santos, R. and I. Quilho: Ourivesaria Portuguesa. Lisbon 1959—60.

Vidal, Manuel Goncalves: Marcas de Contraste e Ourives Portugueses XV° — 1950. Lisbon 1958.

RUMANIA

Until modern times, nothing is known about the hallmarking of objects made of precious metals in Rumania. In Transylvania and Banat, Hungarian regulations were applied until 1919 (see Hungary, also Austria).

1906 — the law of 28 February introduced a modern hallmarking system. Pieces had to be stamped with a purity mark (950, 800 and 750/1000) and a maker's mark.

1919 and 1937 — new marks were introduced, the purity standards being the same as in the 1906 law.

Bibliography:

Nicolescu, C.: Argintăria laică şi religiosă in Tările Române sec. 14.—19. Bucharest 1968.

Tafrali, O.: Le trésor byzantin et roumain du monastère de Poutna. Paris 1925.

RUSSIA

1613 — the first mention of the hallmarking of silver.

1649 — a ban on hallmarking of low purity silver.

1700 — Peter the Great issued a decree on hallmarking not only for Moscow but also for the provinces. After this year the "imenniki" — the maker's marks — appear.

1733 — a decree was issued stipulating the proportion of silver and copper in the alloy: 72 zolotniks of silver and 24 zolotniks of copper.

1729 — first records of the assay office in Moscow.

1735 — an assay office was set up in St Petersburg.

18th—19th centuries — in Moscow the following procedure was followed in marking silver items: the maker stamped his "imennik" on the finished product and then submitted it to the guild where it was marked to indicate that it was of good quality. Then the maker had the item tested in the assay office, where the assayer stamped it with the mark of Moscow and his own mark. In the other towns of the country the objects were marked as follows: 1. town mark, sometimes giving the date; 2. maker's mark with the monogram of his name and sometimes also with the date, always however in a rectangular shield; 3. mark of purity in figures (in zolotniks), always in a rectangular shield.

1891 — uniform marks were introduced for the whole country. The hallmark included the monogram of the assay district administrator, in addition to a depiction of a woman's head.

1927 — a new law on hallmarking came into effect establishing new marks of purity calculated in thousandths.

Bibliography:

Goldberg, T., Mishukov, F., Platonova, N. and Postnikova-Loseva, N. N.: Russkoe zolotoe i serebryanoe delo XV—XX vekov. Moscow 1967.

Rothemund, B.: Verzeichnis der russischen Gold- und Silbermarken. Munich 1971.

SCOTLAND

1457 — James III stipulated the purity of plate silver as 916/1000.

1483 — James III decreed the use of makers' marks.

1489 — the purity standard used in Bruges was adopted.

1525 — the first goldsmiths' guild in Edinburgh.

1555 — renewal of the original Scots purity standard 11 oz (= 916.6/1000).

1681 — introduction of date letters. Letters A to Z were used, excluding J.

1707 — Union of Scotland and England.

Bibliography:

See England.

SPAIN

16th century — a royal decree was issued according to which silver of a purity of 11 dineros 4 granos (= 930/1000) was permitted in producing silver objects. Every goldsmith had to have his own mark. The "marcador" stamped the town mark.

1785 — henceforth the date can be found along with certain town marks.

1881 — commencing with this year the production of silver pieces was liberalized and was usually of lower purity. At the request of the seller or buyer, the purity could be tested by an official assayer (Fiel contraste). Two purities were distinguished: 1. primera ley — no less than 11 dineros = 916/1000; 2. segunda ley = no less than 9 dineros = 750/1000.

1934 — new marks were introduced and purity was determined in thousandths. Items are stamped with two marks: 1. producer's mark; 2. mark of purity.

Bibliography:

Riane, J. F.: The Industrial Arts in Spain. London 1879.
Sanchez, J.: Orfebrería Murciana. 1950.
Sentach, N.: Bosquejo Histórico sobre la orfebrería española. 1908.

SWEDEN

1485 — a letter to the imperial council mentioned stamping items with the maker's mark.

1529 — in the goldsmiths' order of Gustav Vasa the maker's mark was mentioned.

16th century — during this century the maker's mark appeared alongside the town mark.

1689 — the imperial assayer A. Grill, in Stockholm, introduced date letters.

1752 — the state took over the control of the purity of objects made of precious metals.

1758 — the chamber assembly introduced the use of date letters throughout the country (including Finland).

Specimen of hallmarking from this time:

1. town mark (Alingsås); 2. maker's mark (Per Svanander); 3. date letter (for 1782); 4. state control mark.

1860 — instead of marks with the town emblem, special letters were introduced for the different places with assay offices, corresponding to the first letter of the name of the town.

Bibliography:

Upmark, G.: Guld- och Silversmeder i Sverige 1520—1850. Stockholm 1925.

Schwedische Silberschmiederei 1520—1850. Gold- und Silberstempel. Stockholm 1963.

SWITZERLAND

1544 — the administration of Zürich attempted to impose Zürich regulations stipulating the purity of precious metals on the other towns and cantons.

1547 — the proposal of Zürich was adopted in Lucerne and perhaps in Uri, Basel and Solothurn, too.

1848 — the federal government issued a decree on a uniform standard of purity throughout the territory of Switzerland. The individual cantons, however, continued to use their own marks.

1880 — a federal law on the control and guarantee of the purity of silver. Permitted purity 935, 925, 900, 875, and 800/1000.

1882 — uniform marks came into force throughout Switzerland, according to the law of 1880.

1893 — altered marks became valid and were used until 1934. The letter in the shield indicates the seat of the control office.

Bibliography:

Rittmeyer, D. F.: Diverses Etudes sur les Orfèvres Suisses d'Appendzell, Rapperswiller, S. Gallen, Schaffhausen, Toggenburg, etc.

Roosen, Runge M.: Die Goldschmiede der Stadt Bern. Bern 1951.

TUNISIA

1856—1905 — during this period items were stamped with the following marks:

1. mark of purity "Sekka" (c. 900/1000); 2. mark of guarantee "Sahha"; 3. "Khales" mark giving the date.

1878—1905 — introduction of the assayer's mark (a star), stamped on the item when put on sale.

1905 — new marks were introduced on 25 July; permitted purity of 900 and 800/1000. These marks were valid until 1942.

TURKEY

In 1844 a purity of 900/1000 was introduced; previously a purity of 800/1000 was used. An assay was not obligatory, and in any case it was not always precise. From 1923 onwards new marks were introduced, the permitted standards of purity being 900 and 800/1000. The marks changed in 1928, 1938, 1942 while maintaining the same purity standards as of 1923.

U.S.A.

Government bodies, whether colonial, federal or of the individual states, never had any control over the craftsmen and never stipulated purity standards for the use of precious metals. Not even date letters for the item were required. Nonetheless, the cities of New York and Boston had their Societies or Guilds (similar to the European guilds) in which the silversmiths themselves set the standards for their own craft. Most likely other cities of the United States, too, had similar organizations of silversmiths. In Baltimore, in fact, an assay office was set up for precious metals, supervised by elected silversmiths. The marks on American historical silver are mainly those of the makers, consisting either of a monogram or the silversmith's full name. Sometimes this mark is complemented with the name of the place where the maker worked, or a numeral indicating the purity of the precious metal employed. Since no date letter was required, an item can be dated more precisely only by analyzing the decoration on it or by a stylistic appraisal of the entire piece.

Silver objects produced in modern times must have the maker's mark and the number of purity, indicating precisely the purity of the metal with a tolerance of 004/1000. The mark "STERLING" or "STERLING SILVER" indicates a purity of 925/1000.

When identifying American silver it is essential to ascertain precisely and carefully the maker's mark which, in this instance, is the sole reliable indicator since, in many cases, English or Irish products were passed off as American work. Before selling the item the falsifier, of course, removed all the official marks, leaving only that of the maker.

Bibliography:

Avery, L. C.: American Silver of the XVII. and XVIII. Centuries. New York 1920.

Ensko, S. G. C.: American Silversmiths and their Marks. New York 1937.

Graham, J., Jr.: Early American Silvermarks. New York 1936.

Thorn, C. J.: Handbook of American Silver and Pewter Marks. New York 1949.

YUGOSLAVIA

1834 — obligatory hallmarking was introduced in the former Kingdom of Serbia for items manufactured of precious metals.

1882 — the law of 17 July introduced a new system of hallmarking on the territory of the former Kingdom of Serbia with the establishment of provincial control offices. Permitted purities were 800 and 750/1000.

1919 — with the emergence of present-day Yugoslavia, new hallmarks were introduced, valid for the entire country. Permitted purities are 900, 800 and 750/1000.

1933 — new hallmarks were introduced along with new purity standards of 950, 900 and 800/1000.

TABLE OF FORMER PURITY INDICATIONS:

1 lot = 062.5/1000	1 denier = 083.3/1000
12 lots = 750/1000	8 deniers = 666.6/1000
13 lots = 812.5/1000	9 deniers = 750/1000
14 lots = 875/1000	10 deniers = 833.3/1000
15 lots = 937,5/1000	11 deniers = 916.6/1000
16 lots = 1000/1000	12 deniers = 1000/1000

1 zolotnik = 010.4/1000	24 granos = 1 dinero
84 zolotniks = 875/1000	9 dineros = 750/1000
94 zolotniks = 980/1000	11 dineros = 916.6/1000
96 zolotniks = 1000/1000	12 dineros = 1000/1000

20 dwt (pennyweight) = 1 oz (ounce) Troy
11 oz 2 dwt = 925/1000 = Sterling Standard
11 oz 10 dwt = 958.3/1000 = Britannia Standard
12 oz 0. dwt = 1000/1000

Advice to readers:

1. Look for the mark according to what it depicts. Carefully identify, and if uncertain as to the depiction, compare it with similar subjects. Bear in mind that hallmarks usually have many variations which may differ from one another in minor details, and that in the course of time they may have become difficult to decipher. There are also many hallmarks showing several items or motifs. When deciphering the marks, therefore, take careful note of everything they contain.
2. When you have identified the mark with the help of this book, look at the hallmarking system of that particular country at the beginning of the book. An object usually bears more than one mark, the exact number corresponding to local regulations. You can then be certain that you have identified it correctly.
3. Next to each town or area the name of the country to which it now belongs is given. The present situation has been strictly adhered to because the borders of countries were often extremely fluid in historical times and some towns or territories changed hands many times. The names of the towns are given as they are used today, and the historical names appear in brackets.
4. International research on silver hallmarks has by no means ended, and therefore modern specialized literature is not uniform either as to the details of the marks or their dating. The author had no choice but to always keep to a single source which he regarded as the most important.

PLATES

ABBREVIATIONS OF STATES:

A	=	Austria
B	=	Belgium
BG	=	Bulgaria
CH	=	Switzerland
CZ	=	Czech Republic
D	=	Germany
DK	=	Denmark
E	=	Spain
EIR	=	Ireland
ET	=	Egypt
F	=	France
GB	=	Great Britain
H	=	Hungary
I	=	Italy
N	=	Norway
NL	=	Nerherlands
P	=	Portugal
PL	=	Poland
R	=	Romania
S	=	Sweden
SF	=	Finland
SK	=	Slovakia
TN	=	Tunisia
USA	=	United States of America

LETTER A

1 
2 

PARMA (I), 1818—1872,
larger and smaller items

3 

PARIS (F), 1684—1697,
contremarque — small items

4 

AURICH (D), 19th century

5 

BELGIUM, 1869—1942,
state mark of purity 900/1000, smaller items

6 

BELGIUM, 1869—1942,
state mark of purity 800/1000, smaller items

7 

BELGIUM, 1869—1942,
state mark of purity 900/1000, larger items

8 

BELGIUM, 1869—1942,
state mark of purity 800/1000, larger items

9 

PARIS (F), "maison commune" for 1764

10 

PARIS (F), 1744—1750,
charge

11 

AUDENARDE (Oudenaarde) (B), from the beginning of 18th century

12		PARIS (F), "maison commune" for 1644
13		PARIS (F), 1750—1756, *charge*
14		PARIS (F), 1704—1712, *charge*
15		PARIS (F), 1727—1732, *charge*
16		PARIS (F), 1727—1732, *charge*
17		PARIS-GÉNÉRALITÉ (F), (revenue district), 1756—1762, *charge*
18		PARIS (F), 1768—1774, *charge — large items*
19		PARIS-GÉNÉRALITÉ (F), (revenue district), 1756—1762, *charge*
20		PARIS-GÉNÉRALITÉ (F), (revenue district), 1780—1791, *charge*
21		PARIS (F), 1713—1717, *charge*

22 

PARIS (F), 1756—1762, *charge — large items*

23 

PARIS (F), 1713—1717, *charge*

24 

PARIS (F), 1738—1744, *charge*

25 

PARIS (F), 1762—1768, *charge — large items*

26 

PARIS-GÉNÉRALITÉ (F), (revenue district), 1780—1791, *charge —* large items

27 

PARIS (F), 1781—1789, *charge — large items*

28 

PARIS (F), 1775—1781, *charge — large items*

29 

PARIS (F), 1783, *charge — large items*

30 

PARIS (F), 1732—1738, *charge*

31 

PARIS (F), 1722—1727, *charge — large items*

32		PARIS (F), 1717—1722, *charge*
33		METZ (F), 1780—1791, *charge — large items*
34		METZ (F), 1774—1780, *charge — large items*
35		PARIS (F), 1704—1712, *décharge*
36		PARIS (F), 1713—1717, *décharge*
37		SALINS (F), 1784
38		PARIS (F), 1684—1687, *small items*
39		PARIS (F), 1687—1691, *charge — large items*
40		PARIS (F), 1691—1698, *décharge*
41		PARIS (F), 1691—1698, *décharge — small items*

42		PARIS (F), 1691—1698, *charge*
43		**PARIS (F), 1697—1703,** ***charge — large items***
44		ROUEN (F), 1780—1789, *charge — minor items*
45		PARIS (F), 1687—1691, *control mark*
46		VÄSTERÅS (S), 17th—19th centuries
47		PARIS (F), 1684—1687, *contremarque — larger items*
48		PARIS (F), 1684—1687, *older items*
49		PARIS (F), 1677—1680, *charge — large items*
50		PARIS (F), 1680—1684, *charge — large items*
51		MANTES (F), 1748

52 

PARIS (F), 1684—1687, *charge — large items*

53 

PARIS (F), 1684—1687, *charge — small items*

54 

PARIS (F), 1677—1680, *charge — large items*

55 

MEAUX (F), 1750

56 
57 
58 

HUNGARY, 1937—1965, *export mark;*
purity 935/1000
purity 900/1000
purity 800/1000

59 

ALINGSÅS (S), mid-18th century

60 

U.S.A., Abel Buel, 1742—1825, *New Haven, Conn.*

61 

U.S.A., Adrien Bancker, 1703—1772, *New York, N. Y.*

62 

ABERDEEN (GB), 17th—18th centuries, *many variations*

63 

ABERDEEN (GB), 18th century, *many variations*

64		U.S.A., Arnold Collins, 1690 *Newport, R.I.*
65		U.S.A., Alexander Camman, 1813, *Albany, N.Y.*
66		U.S.A., Albert Cole, 1844, *New York, N.Y.*
67		CAEN (F), 1780— 1791, *charge — minor items*
68		MONS (Bergen) (B), 17th—18th centuries
69		SPAIN, from 1934, *export mark*
70		AGUILAR (E), 17th century
71		U.S.A., Abraham Portram, 1727, *New York, N.Y.*
72		L'AQUILA (I), 15th century
73		L'AQUILA (I), 16th century
74		U.S.A., Richard Andras, 1797, *New York, N.Y.*

75  AARHUS (DK), 17th century

76  BAYONNE (F), 1780—1789, *charge — minor items*

77  AMIENS (F), 1780—1790, *charge — minor items*

78  U.S.A., Andrew Tyler, 1692—1741, *Boston, Mass.*

79
80   FORMER AUSTRO-HUNGARIAN EMPIRE, 1872—1902, *import mark*

Key to the Marks:
A — Vienna (A)
B — Linz (A)
C — Prague (CZ)
D — Brno (CZ)
E — Cracow (PL)
F — Lvov ((Ukraine)
G — Graz (A)
H — Bregenz (A)
K — Klagenfurt (A)
L — Ljubljana (Slovenia)
M — Trieste (I)
P — Pest (H)
R — Košice (SK)
T — Timişoara (R)
U — Alba Iulia (R)
V — Zagreb (Croatia)

LETTER B

81
82   PIACENZA (I), 1818—1872, *larger and smaller items*

83 

BAMBERG (D), 17th—18th centuries

84 

FORMER AUSTRO-HUNGARIAN EMPIRE, 1806—1809, *restamped mark for small items*

Key to the Marks:
A — Vienna (A)
B — Prague (CZ)
C — Salzburg (A)
D — Lvov (Ukraine)
E — Cracow (PL)
F — Brno (CZ)
G — Linz (A)
H — Graz (A)
I — Klagenfurt (A)
K — Ljubljana (Slovenia)
L — Trieste (I)

85 

BRZEG (Brieg) (PL), 18th century

86 

BRUGES (B), c. 1660

87 

BORÅS (S), 1745

88 

U.S.A., Thanvet Besley, 1727, *New York, N.Y.*

89 

BESANÇON (F), 18th century

90 

ROUEN (F), 1698, *charge*

91  PAU (F), 18th century

92  TROYES (F), 1774—1780

93  PARIS (F), "maison commune" for 1765

94  PARIS (F), "maison commune" for 1695

95  SENS (F), 1749

96  PARIS (F), "maison commune" for 1670

97  PARIS (F), "maison commune" for 1742

98  ROUEN (F), 1698, *charge*

99  BORDEAUX (F), 1780—1789, *charge — minor items*

100  BOURGES (F) 1780—1789, *charge — minor items*

101		ROUEN (F), 1780—1789, *charge — large items*
102		ROUEN (F), 1774—1780, *charge — large items*
103		PARIS (F), "maison commune" for 1507
104		ROUEN (F), 1768—1774, *charge*
105		BESANÇON (F), late 17th century
106		MANTES (F), 1756
107		ETAMPES (F), 1762
108		VERSAILLES (F), 1746
109		BRAGA (P), 1886—1888
110		BARCELONA (E), 16th—17th centuries

111 

BARCELONA (E), 16th—17th centuries

112 

BARCELONA (E), 15th century

113 

U.S.A., Garrett Onclebagh, 1698, *New York, N.Y.*

114 

U.S.A., Benjamin Hiller, 1687, *Boston, Mass.*

115 

U.S.A., Benjamin Hurd, 1739—1781, *Boston, Mass.*

116 

U.S.A., John Brevoort, 1715—1775, *New York, N.Y.*

117 

U.S.A., Bartholomew Le Roux, 1688—1713, *New York, N.Y.*

118 

U.S.A., Brower and Rusher, 1834, *New York, N.Y.*

119 

BREVIK (N), 18th century

120 

BURGOS (E), 16th century

121 

U.S.A., Barnebus Webb, 1762, *Boston, Mass.*

122 

U.S.A., B. Ward, 1729—1777, *Guilford, Conn.*

123 

U.S.A., Beach and Ward, 1789—1795, *Hartford, Conn.*

124 

BOURGES (F), 1774—1780, *charge — minor items*

125 

BORDEAUX (F), 1774—1780, *charge — minor items*

126 

BAMBERG (D), mid-18th century

127 

GALICIA (under the administration of the former Austro-Hungarian Empire). 1787—1806

Key to the Marks:

A — Myślenice (PL)
B — Bochnia (PL)
C — Nowy Sącz (PL)
D — Tarnów (PL)
E — Dukla (PL)
F — Rzeszów (PL)
G — Lesko (PL)
H — Sambor (Ukraine)
I — Przemyśl (PL)
K — Zamość (PL)
L — Zholkiev (Ukraine)
M — Brody (Ukraine)
N — Lvov (Ukraine)
O — Berezhany (Ukraine)
P — Stry (Ukraine)
Q — Ivano-Frankovsk (Stanislav) (Ukraine)
R — Zaleshchiki (Ukraine)
S — Ternopol (Ukraine)
T — Chernovtsy (1789—1806) (Ukraine)

LETTER C

128 

KULMBACH (D), 16th—17th centuries

129		KARLSTAD (S), 18th—19th centuries
130		CAEN (F), 1744—1750, *charge — large items*
131		PARIS (F), "maison commune" for 1743
132		BESANÇON (F), 1764
133		CAEN (F), 1744—1780, *charge — large items*
134		CAEN (F), 1730—1791, *charge — large items*
135		KRISTIANSTAD (S), 18th—19th centuries
136		OSLO (former Kristiania) (N), 1624—c. 1820, *the numeral signifies the year, here 1747; after 1712 the full date is sometimes given*
137		CALATAYUD (E), 16th century
138		CASTELLÓN DE LA PLANA (E), 16th—17th centuries
139		U.S.A., Charles Le Roux, 1689—1745, *New York, N.Y.*

140 

U.S.A., Charles Candell, 1795, *New York, N.Y.*

141 

U.S.A., Charters, Cann and Dunn, 1850, *New York, N.Y.*

142 
CERVANTES or CERVERA (E) 15th—17th centuries

143 
CAEN (F), 1774—1780, *charge — minor items*

144 

U.S.A., Cornelius Kiersteade, 1753, *New York, N.Y.*

145 

LARVIK (N), 18th century

146 

U.S.A., Charles L. Boehme, 1774—1868, *Baltimore, Md.*

147 

CÓRDOBA (E), 15th—16th centuries

148 

U.S.A., Cleveland and Post, 1815, *Norwich, Conn.*

149 

U.S.A., Forbes, V. G. Collins, 1816, *New York, N.Y.*

150 
GRENOBLE (F), 1775—1780, *charge — minor items*

LETTER D

151		DESSAU (D), 18th—19th centuries
152		LYON (F), 1688—1703, *charge*
153		PARIS (F), "maison commune" for 1744
154		BESANÇON (F), 1765
155		DIJON (F), 1780—1791, *charge — minor items*
156		LYON (F), 1780—1791, *charge — large items*
157		LYON (F), 1775—1780, *charge — large items*
158		LYON (F), 1762—1768, *charge*
159		LYON (F), 1768—1775, *charge — large items*

160 

LYON (F), 1756—1762, *charge*

161 

LYON (F), 17th century, *charge*

162 

U.S.A., Daniel Boyer, 1726—1779, *Boston, Mass.*

163 

U.S.A., Bayley and Douglas, 1789, *New York, N.Y.*

164 

U.S.A., Dupuy and Sons, 1784, *Philadeplhia, Pa.*

165 

U.S.A., David Jesse, 1670—1705, *Boston, Mass.*

166 

U.S.A., D. Maverick, 1828, *New York, N. Y.*

167 

U.S.A., Downing and Phelps, 1810, *New York, N.Y.*

168 

VERSAILLES (F), 1770

169

LETTER E

ERFURT (D), 16th—18th centuries, *the shield changes shape*

170		TOURS (F), 1768—1774, *charge*
171		PARIS (F), "maison commune" for 1745
172		PARIS (F), "maison commune" for 1721
173		TOURS (F), early 18th century, *charge*
174		TOURS (F), 1751—1756, *charge*
175		PARIS (F), "maison commune" for 1673
176		PARIS (F), "maison commune" for 1649
177		PARIS (F), 1704—1712, *contremarque — review*
178		BESANÇON (F), 1768

179		TOURS (F), 1774—1780, *charge — large items*
180		TOURS (F), 1780—1789, *charge — large items*
181		PARIS (F), 1749—1774, *import mark*
182		PARIS (F), "maison commune" for 1745
183		BESANÇON (F), 1794—1797
184		TOURS (F), 1762—1768, *charge*
185		PARIS (F), 1749—1774, *import mark*
186		EMDEN (D), 1820
187		PARIS (F), "maison commune" for 1511

188		BELGIUM, 1831—1869, *import mark*
189		EKSJÖ (S), early 18th century
190		U.S.A., Ephraim Brasher, 1766, *New York, N.Y.*
191		U.S.A., Esekiel Buer, 1764—1846, *Providence, R.I.*
192		U.S.A., Eliphaz Hart, 1789—1866, *Norwich, Conn.*
193		U.S.A., Eliakim Hitshcock, 1752, *Boston, Mass.*
194		U.S.A., Edgar M. Eoff, 1735—1758, *New York, N.Y.*
195		SWITZERLAND, "Poinçon de Notoriété", imitation of French 18th-century marks
196		U.S.A., Edward Pear, 1836, *Boston, Mass.*
197		U.S.A., Eoff and Phyfe, 1844, *New York, N.Y.*
198		ITALY, 1810—1872, *import mark*

199		ASTORGA (E), 16th century
200		FRANCE, 1798—1809, *import mark for small items*
201		ÉVORA (P), 18th—19th centuries
202		VERSAILLES (F), 1775—1781
203		MELUN (F), 2nd half of 18th century
204		U.S.A., Edward Winslow, 1669—1753, *Boston, Mass.*

LETTER F

205		FORSSA (SF), up to 1943
206		FREIBERG (D), 17th century
207		PARIS (F), "maison commune" for 1746
208		PARIS (F), "maison commune" for 1769

209		FLORENCE (I), 18th century
210		BESANÇON (F), 1767
211		PARIS (F), "maison commune" for 1722
212		ANGERS (F), 1780—1789, *charge*
213		CHARTRES (F), 1747
214		PARIS (F), "maison commune" for 1674
215		PARIS (F), "maison commune" for 1722
216		U.S.A., Fletcher and Bardiner, 1812, *Philadelphia, Pa.*
217		U.S.A., Frost and Mumford, 1810, *Providence, R. I.*
218		U.S.A., Francis Richardson, 1718, *Philadelphia, Pa.*

219		FREDRIKSTAD (N), 2nd half of 17th century
220		PRUSSIA, revenue mark for items manufactured prior to 12 February, 1809
		LETTER G
221		GÄVLE (S), 18th—19th centuries
222		PARIS (F), "maison commune" for 1723
223		GHENT (B), 18th century
224		GOTHA (D), 17th century
225		GÖTEBORG (S), 19th century
226		POITIERS (F), 1680
227		PARIS (F), "maison commune" for 1675

228		GUIMARÃES (P), late 18th century
229		POITIERS (F), 1774—1780, *charge — large items*
230		POITIERS (F), 1755
231		POITIERS (F), 1780—1791, *charge — large items*
232		GÄVLE (S), late 17th century
233		GRENOBLE (F), 1780—1791, *charge — minor items*
234		U.S.A., George Bardick, 1790, *Philadelphia, Pa.*
235		GÖTEBORG (S), 17th—18th centuries
236		GERONA (E), 16th century
237		U.S.A., George Hanners, 1697, *Boston, Mass.*

238

U.S.A., Gabriel Lewyn, 1771, *Baltimore, Md.*

239

U.S.A., George Stephens, 1790, *New York, N.Y.*

240

U.S.A., George Tyler, 1740—1785, *Boston, Mass.*

241

GÖRLITZ (D), 18th century

242

PARIS-GÉNÉRALITÉ (F), (revenue district), 1781—1790, *charge — minor items*

LETTER H

243

HÄRNÖSAND (S), 18th—19th centuries

244

HÄRNÖSAND (S), 18th—19th centuries

245

PARIS (F), "maison commune" for 1771

246

PARIS (F), "maison commune" for 1724

247

LA ROCHELLE (F), 1780—1791, *charge — large items*

248		LA ROCHELLE (F), 1774—1780, *charge — large items*
249		HAPARANDA (S), 19th century
250		U.S.A., Henry Andrews, 1795, *Philadelphia, Pa.*
251		HEILBRONN (D), early 18th century
252		U.S.A., Henricus Boelen, 1684—1755, *New York, N.Y.*
253		U.S.A., Henry Hurst, 1665—1717, *Boston, Mass.*
254		U.S.A., Hall and Hewson, 1819, *Albany, N. Y.*
255		U.S.A., Henry Loring, 1773—1818, *Boston, Mass.*
256		U.S.A., Hays and Myers, 1770, *New York, N. Y.*
257		U.S.A., Henry Pitkin, 1834, *East Hartford, Conn.*
258		U.S.A., Henry R. Traux, 1815, Albany, N.Y.

259  KARKKILA (SF), up to 1943

LETTER I

260  IISALMI (SF), up to 1943

261  PARIS (F), 1677—1680, *charge — large items*

262  PARIS (F), "maison commune" for 1725

263  LIMOGES (F), 1774—1780, *charge — large items*

264  LIMOGES (F), 1780—1791, *charge — large items*

265  U.S.A. I. Adam, 1800, *Alexandria, Va.*

266  U.S.A., John Benjamin, 1731—1796, *Stratford, Conn.*

267  U.S.A., John Burt, 1691—1745, *Boston, Mass.*

268  U.S.A., Jacob Boelen, 1773, *New York, N.Y.*

269 

U.S.A., John Carman, 1771, *Philadelphia, Pa.*

270 

U.S.A., I. Clark, 1754, *Boston, Mass.*

271 

U.S.A., John Coney, 1655—1722, *Boston, Mass.*

272 

U.S.A., John Coney, 1655—1722, *Boston, Mass.*

273 

U.S.A., John Coddington, 1690—1743, *Newport, R.I.*

274 

U.S.A., John Dixwell, 1680—1725, *Boston, Mass.*

275 

U.S.A., John David, 1736—1794, *Philadelphia, Pa.*

276 

U.S.A., Jonathan Davenport, 1789—1801, *Baltimore, Md.*

277 

U.S.A., John Edwards, 1700, *Boston, Mass.*

278 

U.S.A., John Edwards, 1700, *Boston, Mass.*

279		U.S.A., Joseph Goldthwaite, 1706—1780, *Boston, Mass.*
280		U.S.A., Jacob B. Lansing, 1736, *Albany, N.Y.*
281		U.S.A., John Hull, 1624—1683, *Boston, Mass.*
282		U.S.A., John Hastier, 1726, *New York, N.Y.*
283		U.S.A., John Inch, 1720—1763, *Annapolis, Md.*
284		IKAALINEN (SF), up to 1943
285		U.S.A., Joseph Keeler, 1786—1824, *Norwalk, Conn.*
286		ILMAJOKI (SF), up to 1943
287		U.S.A., John Lyng, 1734, *Philadelphia, Pa.*
288		U.S.A., John Denise, 1698, *Philadelphia, Pa.*
289		U.S.A., John Noyes, 1695, *Boston, Mass.*

290 

FORMER CZECHOSLOVAKIA, inventory mark of 1929, *for purity 950—650/1000*

291 

U.S.A., Isaac Perkins, 1707, *Charlestown, Mass.*

292 

U.S.A., Jonathan Reed, 1725—1740, *Boston, Mass.*

293 

U.S.A., Isaiah Wagster, 1776—1793, *Baltimore, Md.*

LETTER J

294 

U.S.A., Joseph Anthony and Sons, 1810, *Philadelphia, Pa.*

295 

U.S.A., John Boyce, 1801, *New York, N.Y.*

296 

U.S.A., Jonathan Crosby, 1743—1769, *Boston, Mass.*

297 

U.S.A., John Denise, 1798, *New York, N. Y.*

298 

DIJON (F), 1774—1780, *charge — minor items*

299 

U.S.A., Joseph Moulton II, 1757, *Newburyport, Mass.*

300 

U.S.A., Joseph Phillipe, 1796, *Baltimore, Md.*

301 

U.S.A., Joseph P. Warner, 1811—1862, *Baltimore, Md.*

302 

U.S.A., John Starr Blackman, 1777—1851, *Danbury, Conn.*

303 

U.S.A., John Wendover, 1694, *New York, N.Y.*

304 

U.S.A., Joseph W. Boyd, 1820, *New York, N.Y.*

305 

U.S.A., J. W. Faulkner, 1835, *New York, N.Y.*

LETTER K

306 

KARLSHAMN (S), 1st half of 18th century

307 

PARIS (F), "maison commune" for 1750

308 

PARIS (F), "maison commune" for 1773

309 

PARIS (F), "maison commune" for 1726

310 

BORDEAUX (F), 1744—1750, *charge*

311 

PARIS (F), 1677—1680, *charge — large items*

312 

KØGE (DK), 18th century

313 

LILLE (F), 1750, *date letter*

314 

LILLE (F), 1776

315 

BORDEAUX (F), 1756—1762, *charge*

316 

BORDEAUX (F), 1738—1744, *charge*

317
318  

BORDEAUX (F), 1768—1774, *charge*

319 

PARIS (F), "maison commune" for 1726

320		BORDEAUX (F), 1698—1703, *charge*
321		BORDEAUX (F), 1774—1780, *charge*
322		BORDEAUX (F), 1780—1789, *charge — large items*
323		PARIS (F), "maison commune" for 1515
324		BORDEAUX (F), 1672—1680, *charge*
325		KUNGSBACKA (S), 18th—19th centuries
326		U.S.A., Krider and Biddle, 1830, *Philadelphia, Pa.*
327		U.S.A., Koenraet Ten Eyck, 1678—1735, *New York, N.Y.*
328		BORDEAUX (F), 1691—1698, *charge*
329		KIEV (Ukraine), 1735—1774

330 

KOTKA (SF), up to 1943

331 

KASKINEN (SF), up to 1943

LETTER L

332 

LIEKSA (SF) and LOHJA (SF), up to 1943

333 

LOVIISA (SF), up to 1943

334 

LEIPZIG (D), 16th century up to the beginning of 18th century, many variations

335 

OŁAWA (Ohlau) (PL), 17th—18th centuries

336 

LISBON (P), 1881—1887, *minimum purity 750/1000*

337 

LISBON (P), 1881—1887, *minimum purity 750/1000*

338 

PARIS (F), "maison commune" for 1752

339 

LISBON (P), 18th—19th centuries

340

LISBON (P), late 17th century

341

LISBON (P), 17th—18th centuries

342

BAYONNE (F), 1774—1780, *charge — large items*

343

LYON (F), 1780—1791, *charge — minor items*

344

TOURS (F), 1738—1744, *charge*

345

BAYONNE (F), mid-18th century

346

LAPUA (SF), up to 1943

347

U.S.A., Loring Bailey, 1780, *Hingham, Mass.*

348

LEÓN (E), 18th century

349

U.S.A., Lincoln and Green, 1810, *Boston, Mass.*

350  LAHTI (SF), up to 1943

351  BAYONNE (F), 1780—1789, *charge — large items*

352  VERSAILLES (F), 1780—1789 *charge — large items*

353  LOIMAA (SF), up to 1943

354  POTSDAM (D), 18th century, *mark of purity*

355  U.S.A., Lemuel Wells, 1791, *New York, N.Y.*

356  POITIERS (F), 1774—1780, *charge — minor items*

357  LA ROCHELLE (F), 1774—1780, *charge — small items*

358  VERSAILLES (F), 1780—1789, *charge — medium-sized items*

359  LIMOGES (F), 1780—1791, *charge — minor items*

360  PARIS (F), 1783, *charge — minor items*

361  PARIS (F), 1781—1789, *charge — medium-sized items*

362  LISBON (P), 1886—1888

LETTER M

363  MAARIANHAMINA (SF), up to 1943

364  MALMKÖPING (S), 19th century

365  TOULOUSE (F), 16th—17th centuries, *charge*

366  PARIS (F), "maison commune" for 1775

367  PARIS (F), "maison commune" for 1752

368
369   MEXICO, 1770, *throughout the Spanish occupation*

370  TOULOUSE (F), 16th—17th centuries, *charge*

371
372   PALMA DE MALLORCA (E), 1881—1934, *for large items, for small items*

373  METZ (F), 1780—1791, *charge — small items*

374  TOULOUSE (F), 1768—1774, *charge*

375  TOULOUSE (F), 1768—1774, *charge*

376  TOULOUSE (F), 1774—1780, *charge — large items*

377  TOULOUSE (F), 1780—1789, *charge — large items*

378  TOULOUSE (F), 16th—17th centuries, *charge*

379  PARIS (F), "maison commune" for 1517

380 

ANGERS (F), 1768—1774, *charge*

381 

MANTES (F), 1743

382 

TOULOUSE (F), 16th—17th centuries, *charge*

383 

MALTA, 1623—1636

384 

MEAUX (F), 1750, *middle letter changes according to year*

385 

MEAUX (F), 1768, *middle letter changes according to year*

386 

MEAUX (F), 1778, *middle letter changes according to year*

387 

388 

FORMER AUSTRO-HUNGARIAN EMPIRE, 1887, *hallmark for low sub-standard purity*

389 

MARIEFRED (S), 18th century

390 

U.S.A., Munson Jarvis, 1742—1824, *Stamford, Conn.*

391 

U.S.A., Mathias Lamar, 1790, *Philadelphia, Pa.*

392 

U.S.A., Marcus Merriman and Co., 1817, *New Haven, Conn.*

393 

U.S.A., McFee and Reeder, 1796, *Philadelphia, Pa.*

394 

METZ (F), 1774—1780, *charge — minor items*

395 

AMIENS (F), 1774—1780, *charge — minor items*

396 

LIMOGES (F), 1774—1780, *charge — minor items*

397 

ORLÉANS (F), 1780—1791, *charge — minor items*

398 

LYON (F), 1775—1780, *charge — minor items*

399 

BAYONNE (F), 1774—1780, *charge — minor items*

LETTER N

400 

NUREMBERG (D), 1700—1750

401 

PARIS (F), "maison commune" for 1682

402 

PARIS (F), "maison commune" for 1753

403 

NUREMBERG (D), 19th century

404 

PARIS (F), "maison commune" for 1729

405 

NUREMBERG (D), up to mid-16th century

406 

NANTES (F), 1762—1769, *charge*

407 

NANTES (F), 1769—1784, *charge*

408 

NAPLES (I), 18th century, *changing date, here 1716*

409  NAPLES (I), 16th century,

410  NÆSTVED (DK), 17th—18th centuries

411  U.S.A., Nathaniel Morse, 1709, *Boston, Mass.*

LETTER O

412  OSTERODE (D), 17th—18th centuries

413  PARIS (F), "maison commune" for 1707

414  PARIS (F), "maison commune" for 1777

415  RIOM (F), 1774—1780, *charge — large items*

416  RIOM (F), 1780—1789, *charge — large items*

417  MONTEREAU (F), 1768—1774, *contremarque*

418		OSTERODE (D), 19th century
419		OCHSENFURT (D), 17th century
420		U.S.A., Otto Paul De Parisien, 1763, *New York, N.Y.*
421		U.S.A., O. Parisien and Son, 1789, *New York, N.Y.*
422		ORLÉANS (F), 1774—1780, *charge — minor items*
423		TOURS (F), 1774—1780, *charge — minor items*
424		RIOM (F), 1774—1780, *charge — minor items*
		LETTER P
425		OPORTO (P), 18th century
426		OPORTO (P), mid-16th century
427		DIJON (F), 1756—1759, *charge*

428		NANTES (F), 1746, *charge*
429		OPORTO (P), 1881—1887, *minimum purity 750/1000*
430		OPORTO (P), 1886—1888
431		OPORTO (P), since 1891, *control mark for silver watches*
432		PARIS (F), "maison commune" for 1789
433		PARIS (F), "maison commune" for 1788
434		DIJON (F), 1775—1780, *charge — large items*
435		DIJON (F), 1780—1791, *charge — large items*
436		DIJON (F), 1691—1698, *charge*
437		PARIS (F), "maison commune" for 1788

438  PARIS (F), "maison commune" for 1784

439  DIJON (F), 1756—1759, *charge*

440  DIJON (F), 1759—1762, *charge*

441  PARIS (F), "maison commune" for 1785

442  DIJON (F), 1732—1744, *charge*

443  DIJON (F), 1759—1762, *charge*

444  PARIS (F), "maison commune" for 1786

445  DIJON (F), 1726—1732, *charge*

446  PARIS (F), "maison commune" for 1787

447  POITIERS (F), 1780—1791, *charge — minor items*

448		DIJON (F), 17th century, *charge*
449		DIJON (F), 1750—1756
450		PARIS (F), "maison commune" for 1787
451		PARIS (F), "maison commune" for 1784
452		PARIS (F), "maison commune" for 1785
453		PARIS (F), "maison commune" for 1786
454		PARIS (F), "maison commune" for 1789
455		PAU (F), early 18th century
456		U.S.A., Phineas Bradley, 1745—1797, *New Haven, Conn.*
457		U.S.A., Peter David, 1707—1755, *Philadelphia, Pa.*

458 

BUDAPEST (H), 19th century, *for silver-plating on pipes*

459 

U.S.A., Peter Feurt, 1731, *New York, N.Y.*

460 

ST PETERSBURG (Russia), 1873—1896, *changing date*

461 

U.S.A., Parry and Musgrave, 1793, *Philadeplhia, Pa.*

462 

U.S.A., Peter Oliver, 1709, *Boston, Mass.*

463 

U.S.A., Peter Perreaux, 1797, *Philadelphia, Pa.*

464 

U.S.A., Peter Quintard, 1731, *New York, N.Y.*

465 

U.S.A., Paul Revere Sr., 1702—1754, *Boston, Mass.*

466 

U.S.A., Paul Revere, 1735—1818, *Boston, Mass.*

467 

U.S.A., Paul Revere, 1735—1818, *Boston, Mass.*

468 

U.S.A., Philip Syng, 1703—1789, *Philadelphia, Pa.*

469		PARIS (F), 1775—1781, *charge — small items*
		LETTER Q
470		PARIS (F), "maison commune" for 1709
471		BESANÇON (F), 1777
472		PARIS (F), "maison commune" for 1650
473		PARIS (F), "maison commune" for 1732
		LETTER R
474		PARIS (F), "maison commune" for 1780
475		PARIS (F), "maison commune" for 1733
476		LILLE (F), 1755, *date letter*
477		ORLÉANS (F), 1762, *charge*

478		ROSKILDE (DK), 18th century
479		BESANÇON (F), 1778
480		ORLÉANS (F), 1780—1791, *charge — large items*
481		ORLÉANS (F), 1774—1780, *charge — large items*
482		ORLÉANS (F), 1732, *charge*
483		ORLÉANS (F), 1751—1762, *charge*
484		RENNES (F), 1780—1789, *charge — minor items*
485		RIOM (F), 1780—1789, *charge — minor items*
486		ORLÉANS (F), 1768—1774, *charge*
487		BELGIUM, 1831, *"review" — introduced during transition from the Dutch to the Belgian system of hallmarking*

488		ROSTOCK (D), late 16th century and 17th century
489		BELGIUM, 1831, *"review" — introduced during transition from the Dutch to the Belgian system of hallmarking*
490		U.S.A., Robert Brookhouse, 1750, *Salem, Mass.*
491		U.S.A., Joseph Conyers, 1708, *Boston, Mass.*
492		U.S.A., Robert Douglas, 1776, *New London, Conn.*
493		U.S.A., Rufus Greene, 1707—1777, *Boston, Mass.*
494		U.S.A., Rene Grignon, 1715, *Norwich, Conn.*
495		U.S.A., Riggs and Griffith, 1816, *Baltimore, Md.*
496		ROVANIEMI (SF), up to 1943
497		U.S.A., Robert Sanderson, 1693, *Boston, Mass.*
498		U.S.A., Richard Vincent, 1799, *Baltimore, Md.*

499		U.S.A., Robert Wilson, 1816, *New York, N.Y.*
500		LA ROCHELLE (F), 1780—1791, *charge — minor items*
501		RENNES (F), 1774—1780, *charge — minor items*
502		ROUEN (F), 1774—1780, *charge — minor items*

LETTER S

503		SALZBURG (A), 16th—17th centuries
504		SALZBURG (A), 18th century
505		SKIEN (N), 2nd half of 18th century
506		SKÖVDE (S), 18th century
507		PARIS (F), "maison commune" for 1758
508		PARIS (F), "maison commune" for 1781

509		STOCKHOLM (S), 1500—1600
510		SENLIS (F), 1723
511		PARIS (F), "maison commune" for 1734
512		LILLE (F), 1755, *date letter*
513		SCHWEINFURT (D), 18th century
514		SURSEE (CH), 17th—18th centuries
515		SURSEE (CH), 18th century
516		SURSEE (CH), early 17th century
517		U.S.A., Samuel Avery, 1760—1836, *Preston, Conn.*
518		SAKSKØBING (DK), c. 1696

519 

TURKEY, 1928—1938, purity 900/1000

520 

TURKEY, 1928—1938, purity 800/1000

521 

U.S.A., Samuel Burt, 1724—1754, *Boston, Mass.*

522 

U.S.A., Samuel Burrill, 1733, *Boston, Mass.*

523 

U.S.A., Chaudrons, Simon and Co., 1807, *Philadelphia, Pa.*

524 

U.S.A., Storrs and Cooley, 1832, *New York, N.Y.*

525 

U.S.A., Shem Drowne, 1749, *Boston, Mass.*

526 

U.S.A., Stephen Emory, 1725—1801, *Boston, Mass.*

527 

U.S.A., Samuel Gilbert, 1798, *Hebron, Conn.*

528 

U.S.A., Samuel Haugh, 1675—1717, *Boston, Mass.*

529 

U.S.A., Jacobus van de Spiegel, 1668—1708, *New York, N. Y.*

530  U.S.A., Vanderspiegel, 1701, *New York, N.Y.*

531  U.S.A., Samuel Leach, 1741, *Philadelphia, Pa.*

532  U.S.A., Samuel Minott, 1732—1803, *Boston, Mass.*

533  U.S.A., Sibley and Marble, 1801—1806, *New Haven, Conn.*

534  U.S.A., Simon Sexnine, 1722, *New York, N.Y.*

535  VIENNA (A), 1774—1776, *items of sub-standard purity*

536  STEGE (DK), c. 1750

537  STELLA (I), 15th—16th centuries

538  SULMONA (I), since 13th century, *the stamp changes shape*

539  SUHL (D), 17th—18th centuries

540  U.S.A., Samuel Williamson, 1794, *Philadelphia, Pa.*

541		BORDEAUX (F), 1687—1691, *charge*
542		PRAGUE (CZ), 1776—1806, *for sub-standard purity*
543		TOULOUSE (F), 1774—1780, *charge — minor items*
544		ST-GERMAIN (F), 1781, *charge — medium-sized items*
545		ST-GERMAIN (F), 1781, *charge — large items*

LETTER T

546		TORGAU (D), 16th—17th centuries
547		TAMPERE (SF), up to 1943
548		PARIS (F), "maison commune" for 1735
549		PARIS (F), "maison commune" for 1782

550		NANTES (F), 1744, *charge*
551		TOURNAI (Doornijk) (B), 1st half of 17th century
552		SALINS (F), 1779
553		TOURNAI (Doornijk) (B), 2nd half of 18th century
554		TOURNAI (Doornijk) (B), 2nd half of 18th century
555		TOURS (F), 1780—1789, *charge — minor items*
556		U.S.A., Timothy Bontecou Jr., 1723—1789, *New Haven, Conn.*
557		U.S.A., Trott and Brooks, 1798, *New London, Conn.*
558		U.S.A., Thomas Carson, 1815, *Albany, N.Y.*
559		U.S.A., Timothy Dwight, 1645—1691, *Boston, Mass.*

560		FORMER AUSTRO-HUNGARIAN EMPIRE, 1810—1824, *tax mark for smaller items (confirmation of payment of special fee)*
561 562	 	FORMER AUSTRO-HUNGARIAN EMPIRE, 1809—1810, *exemption mark for smaller items (exempt from consignment to State Treasury)*
563		FORMER AUSTRO-HUNGARIAN EMPIRE, 1809—1810, *exemption mark for larger items (exempt from consignment to State Treasury)*
564		FORMER AUSTRO-HUNGARIAN EMPIRE, 1810—1824, *tax mark for larger items (confirmation of payment of special fee) for significance of letter see mark No 1901*
565		ZELENOGORSK (Terijoki) (Russia), up to 1943
566		U.S.A., Thomas Knox Emery, 1781—1815, *Boston, Mass.*
567		U.S.A., Thomas Millner, 1690—1745, *Boston, Mass.*
568		TOULOUSE (F), 1780—1789, *charge, minor items*
569		TOLEDO (E), 17th century

570 

TOLEDO (E), c. 1600

571 

U.S.A., Thomas Skinner, 1712—1761, *New York, N.Y.*

572 

U.S.A., Thomas Sparrow, 1764—1784, *Annapolis, Md.*

573 

U.S.A., Thomas Townshendt, 1727, *Boston, Mass.*

574 

TUNISIA, 1904, *review*

575 

U.S.A., Thomas You, 1756, *Charleston, S.C.*

LETTER U

576 

UUSIKIRKKO (SF), up to 1943

577 

ULRICEHAMN (S), 18th—19th centuries

578 

PARIS (F), "maison commune" for 1783

LETTER V

579 

PARIS (F), "maison commune" for 1760

580		SENLIS (F), 1747
581		LILLE (F), 1732, *date letter*
582		TROYES (F), 1772, *charge*
583		VIRTON (B), 18th century
584		PARIS (F), "maison commune" for 1655
585		TROYES (F), 1774—1780, *charge?*
586		PARIS (F), "maison commune" for 1736
587		TROYES (F), 1768—1774, *charge*
588		U.S.A., Peter van Dyke, 1684—1750, *New York, N.Y.*
589		U.S.A., Nicholas Roosevelt, 1745—1769, *New York, N.Y.*

590
591

FORMER AUSTRO-HUNGARIAN EMPIRE, 1810—1824, *inventory mark for items manufactured after 1810*

592

KOMÁRNO (SK), KOMÁROM (H), from 17th century to the end of 18th century

593

U.S.A., van Ness and Waterman, 1835, *New York, N.Y.*

LETTER W

594

VIIPURI (SF), up to 1943

595

VISBY (S), 18th century

596

WROCŁAW (PL), 2nd half of 17th century up to c. 1740

597

WEIMAR (D), early 17th century

598

VISBY (S), 19th century

599

VÄXJÖ (S), 18th—19th centuries

600

VEVEY (CH), 18th century

601		LILLE (F), 1780—1789, *reconnaissance*
602		VAMMALA (SF), up to 1943
603		VARBERG (S), early 18th century
604		U.S.A., William B. North, 1787—1838, *New York, N.Y.*
605		U.S.A., William Clark, 1774, *New Milford, Conn.*
606		U.S.A., William Cross, 1712, *Boston, Mass.*
607		U.S.A., W. M. Cowel, 1682—1736, *Boston, Mass.*
608		U.S.A., William Paris, 1728—1804, *Annapolis, Md.*
609		U.S.A., William Gale, 1816, *New York, N.Y.*
610		U.S.A., Woodward and Grosjean, 1847, *Boston, Mass.*
611		U.S.A., William Huertin, 1731—1771, *New York, N.Y.*
612		U.S.A., William Homes, 1717—1783, *Boston, Mass.*

613 

U.S.A., William Hollingshead, 1770, *Philadelphia, Pa.*

614 

U.S.A., Wood and Hughes, 1846, *New York, N.Y.*

615 

U.S.A., Benjamin Wynkoop, 1675—1751, *New York, N.Y.*

616 

U.S.A., William McParlin, 1780—1850, *Maryland*

617 

U.S.A., William Rouse, 1639—1705, *Boston, Mass.*

618 

U.S.A., Pelletreau and Richards, 1825, *New York, N.Y.*

619 

U.S.A., William Vilant, 1725, *Philadelphia, Pa.*

620 

U.S.A., William Whetcroft, 1735—1799, *Baltimore, Md.*

621 

U.S.A., William Ward, 1742—1828, *Lichtfield, Conn.*

622 

U.S.A., W.W. Gaskins, 1830, *Providence, R.I.*

LETTER X

623 

PARIS (F), "maison commune" for 1690

624		PARIS (F), "maison commune" for 1714
625		PARIS (F), "maison commune" for 1761
626		PARIS (F), "maison commune" for 1666
627		BESANÇON (F), 1782
628		AMIENS (F), 1774—1780, *charge — large items*
629		AMIENS (F), 1780—1791, *charge — large items*
630		EXETER (GB), 1575—1698, *several variations*
631		PARIS (F), 1691—1698, *contremarque — small items*
632 633 634		BESANÇON (F), first third of 18th century
635 636		BESANÇON (F), 1674—1689

637 638

BESANÇON (F), late 18th century

639

KARLSKRONA (S), 17th—18th centuries

640

BESANÇON (F), 17th century

641 642

AMIENS (F), 1768—1774, *charge — large items*

LETTER Y

643

PARIS (F), "maison commune" for 1692

644

SALINS (F), 1759

645

BOURGES (F), 1780—1789, *charge — large items*

646

BOURGES (F), 1774—1780, *charge — large items*

647

VERSAILLES (F), 1780

648  IEPER (Ypres) (B), 2nd half of 17th century

649  BOURGES (F), 1768—1774, *charge — minor items*

650  IEPER (YPRES) (B), 1701—1713

LETTER Z

651  ZÜRICH (CH), 17th century

652  MANNHEIM (D), 17th—18th centuries

653  ZERBST (D), 18th century, *different varieties of shields*

654  PARIS (F), "maison commune" for 1763

655  PARIS (F), "maison commune" for 1643

656  BESANÇON (F), 1730

657  BESANÇON (F), 1783

658  PARIS (F), "maison commune" for 1739

659  NORRKÖPING (S), 17th—18th centuries

660  GRENOBLE (F), 1780—1791, *charge — large items*

661  GRENOBLE (F), 1775—1780, *charge — large items*

662  ZÜRICH (CH), 17th—18th centuries

663  GRENOBLE (F), 1756—1762, *charge*

664  ZITTAU (D), c. 1750

665  ZÜRICH (CH), 17th—18th centuries

666  U.S.A., Zachariah Brigden, 1734—1787, *Boston, Mass.*

LETTER &

667  BESANÇON (F), 1730

668  FRANCE, 1809—1819, *import mark for small items*

669  MILAN (I), 1810—1859, *mark of the guarantee office*

NUMERALS

670  BRAGA (P), 1886—1919, *export mark 800/1000*

671  LISBON (P), 1886—1919, *export mark 800/1000*

672
673   OPORTO (P), 1886—1919, *export mark 800/1000*

674  OPORTO (P), 1919—1938, *export mark*

675  GONDOMAR (P), 1919—1938, *export mark*

676  LISBON (P), 1919—1938, *export mark*

677 

PARIS (F), "maison commune" for 1581

678 
TBILISI (Tiflis) (Georgia), 1830

679 

SPAIN, 1881—1934, *purity 750/1000*

680 
RENNES (F), 1780—1789, *charge — large items*

681 
RENNES (F), 1774—1780, *charge — large items*

682 

BESANÇON (F), 18th century?

683 

FORMER AUSTRO-HUNGARIAN EMPIRE, 1806—1809, *restamped hallmark for large items; for significance of letter see mark No. 1901, here Prague*

684 

TUNISIA, since 1905, *Public Assayer's mark*

685 

COLOGNE (D), mid-18th century

686 

STRASBOURG (F), 2nd half of 18th century

687 

STRASBOURG (F), c. 1650—c. 1750

688 

COLOGNE (D), end of 18th century

689 

WÜRZBURG (D), 18th century

690 

WÜRZBURG (D), 18th century

691 

TRIESTE, 18th century

692 

MANNHEIM (D), 1737—1766

693 

PROVINS (F), 1784—1789

694 

JAPAN, since 1928, *mark of purity in thousandths*

695 

FINLAND, 1810—1972, *mark of purity in thousandths*

HUMAN FIGURES

696 

SKÄNNINGE (S), 18th—19th centuries

697 

TORSHÄLLA (S), 18th century

698 

VELIKY USTYUG (Russia), 1755—1767

699 

VELIKY USTYUG (Russia), 1837—1896

700 

RYAZAN (Russia), 18th and 19th centuries

701 

VELIKY USTYUG (Russia), 1783—1814

702 

KIEV (Ukraine), from 1778 to the beginning of 19th century

703 

KIEV (Ukraine), 1848—1865

704 

SANTIAGO (E), 16th century

705		BRUSSELS (Bruxelles) (B), 1750—c. 1760
706		ASKERSUND (S), 18th century
707		LIDKÖPING (S), 17th—19th centuries
708		UGLICH (Russia), 1762—1778
709		ASKERSUND (S), early 19th century
710		SÖDERTÄLJE (S), 18th—19th centuries
711		MARIEFRED (S), 18th—19th centuries
712		ARKHANGELSK (Russia), 1763—1768
713		ARKHANGELSK (Russia), 1796—1798
714		ARKHANGELSK (Russia), 2nd half of 19th century

715

ARKHANGELSK (Russia), 1880—1890

716

MUNICH (D), c. 1700

717

MUNICH (D), changing date, here 1752

718

MUNICH (D), with two numerals in the date, 1762—1860, *many variations of the shield*

719

GREAT BRITAIN, 1697—1716, *"Britannia"*

720

GREAT BRITAIN, 1716—1717, *"Britannia"*

721

GREAT BRITAIN, 1731—1732, *"Britannia"*

722

GREAT BRITAIN, 1863—1864, *"Britannia"*

723

TORSHÄLLA (S), 19th century

724

NORRKÖPING (S), 18th century

725  VIBORG (DK), 17th—18th centuries

726  BRUSSELS (Bruxelles) (B), early 18th century

727  STOCKHOLM (S), 1600—1700

728  WROCŁAW (PL), from the end of 17th century to 1842, *many variations*

729  WROCŁAW (PL), since 1843, *the numeral changes according to the year*

730  CHARTRES (F), 1768—1774, *contremarque*

731  SENLIS (F), 1784—1789

732  PARIS (F), 1819—1838, *guarantee for medium-sized items*

733  FRANCE — departments, 1798—1809, *guarantee for medium-sized items*

734  FRANCE — departments, 1798—1809, *guarantee for medium-sized items*

735 

PARIS (F), 1793—1794 (1840?), *guarantee of the goldsmiths' guild for silver of any purity (also export mark up to 1840?)*

736 

PARIS (F), 1798—1809, *guarantee for medium-sized items*

737 

PARIS (F), 1798—1809, *guarantee for medium-sized items*

738 

FORMER YUGOSLAVIA, 1882—1919, *purity 800/1000 — large items, valid on the territory of the former Serbian Kingdom*

739 

FORMER YUGOSLAVIA, 1882—1919, *purity 750/1000 — large items, valid on the territory of the former Serbian Kingdom*

740 

PARIS (F), end of 1794—1797, *guarantee of the goldsmiths' guild for purity 958/1000 (also export mark up to 1840?)*

741 

METZ (F), 1774—1780, *décharge — minor items*

742 

BLOIS (F), 1768—1774, *décharge*

743 

SENS (F), 1768—1774, *décharge*

744  DIJON (F), 1780—1791, *décharge — minor items*

745  FRANCE, 1 September—31 October 1809, *"general review", mark for large items*

746  ROUEN (F), 1780—1789, *décharge — minor items*

747 

FRANCE, 1798—1809, *import mark for large items*

748  VADSTENA (S), 18th century

749  STOCKHOLM (S), 1720—1740

750  BORDEAUX (F), end of 18th century, *décharge*

751  CAEN (F), 1774—1780, *décharge — large items*

752  BORDEAUX (F), 1774—1780, *décharge — minor items*

753  TROYES (F), 1768—1774, *décharge*

754		PARIS (F), 1781—1789, *décharge — large items*
755		PARIS (F), 1783, *décharge — medium-sized items*
756		PARIS (F), 1781—1789, *décharge — minor items*
757		PARIS (F), 1756—1762, *décharge — large items*
758		FERRARA (I), 17th century
759		POITIERS (F), 1780—1791, *décharge — minor items*
760		ORLÉANS (F), 1780—1791, *décharge — large items*
761		PARIS (F), 1768—1774, *décharge — medium-sized items*
762		PARIS (F), 1781—1789, *décharge — medium-sized items*
763		ORLÉANS (F), 1780—1791, *décharge — minor items*

764 
765 

ORLÉANS (F), 1768—1774, *décharge*

766 

LYON (F), 1762—1768, *décharge — large items*

767 

AMIENS (F), 1768—1774, *décharge*

768 

AMIENS (F), 1774—1780, *décharge — minor items*

769 

BRAGA (P), 1886—1911, *for older items or antiques*

770 

GONDOMAR (P), 1913—1938, *for older items or antiques*

771 

OPORTO (P), 1886—1938, *for older items or antiques*

772 

GONDOMAR (P), 1886—1913, *for older items or antiques*

773 

LISBON (P), 1886—1938, *for older items or antiques*

774 

PARIS (F) 1809—1819, *guarantee for large items*

775 

FRANCE — departments, 1809—1819, *guarantee for large items*

776 

MUNICH (D), 16th—17th centuries

777 

PARIS (F), 1819—1838, *guarantee for large items*

778 

PARIS (F), 9 November 1797 — August(?) 1798, *review mark for small items*

779 

FRANCE, 9 November 1797 — August 1798, *general review — mark for large items*

780 

PARIS (F), 1819—1838, *import mark for small items*

781 

PARIS (F), 1 September—31 October 1809, *review mark for large items*

782 

FRANCE — departments, 1819—1838, *guarantee for large items, the numeral in the mark indicates the seat of the assay office, here 84 — Auxerre*

783 

PARIS (F), 1819—1838, *purity 800/1000*

784 

FRANCE — departments, 1819—1838, *purity 800/1000*

785  GREAT BRITAIN, 1784—1786, *duty mark (head of King George III)*

786  GREAT BRITAIN, 1837—1889/90, *duty mark (head of Queen Victoria)*

787  FRANCE — departments, 1840—1879, *export mark*

788  ITALY, 1873—1935, *purity 950/1000*

789  ITALY, 1873—1935, *purity 900/1000*

790  ITALY, 1873—1935, *purity 800/1000*

791  FORMER CZECHOSLOVAKIA, 1921—1928 *purity 950/1000*

792  FORMER CZECHOSLOVAKIA, 1921—1928, *purity 900/1000*

793  FORMER CZECHOSLOVAKIA, 1921—1928, *purity 800/1000*

794  FORMER CZECHOSLOVAKIA, 1921—1928, *purity 750/1000, for larger items*

795
796
797

FORMER YUGOSLAVIA, since 1933, *for large items: purity 950/1000, purity 900/1000, purity 800/1000*

798

LATVIA, c. 1920—c. 1939

799

LATVIA, c. 1920—c. 1939, *purity 875/1000*

800

LATVIA, c. 1920—c. 1939, *import mark, purity 875/1000*

801
802

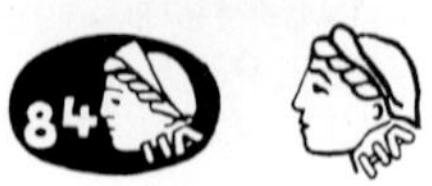

RUSSIA, 1896—1908, *purity 875/1000 (84 zolotniks)*

803

STOCKHOLM (S), 1700—1850

804

STOCKHOLM (S), 1700—1850

805

STOCKHOLM (S), 1700—1850

806

FREISING (D), 18th century

807

LIÈGE (Luik) (B), 1693

808  NAPLES (I), 17th—18th centuries, *changing shield*

809  MEAUX (F), 1774—1780, *décharge*

810  COMPIÈGNE (F), 1768—1774, *contremarque*

811  PARIS (F), 1768—1774, *décharge — large items*

812  GREAT BRITAIN, 1786—1820, *duty mark (head of King George III)*

813  GREAT BRITAIN, 1820—1830, *duty mark (head of King George IV)*

814  GREAT BRITAIN, 1830—1837, *duty mark (head of King William IV)*

815 

FRANCE — departments, 1809—1819, *guarantee for medium-sized items, the numeral in the mark indicates the seat of the assay office, here 25 — Besançon*

816  PARIS (F), 1819—1830, *import mark for large items*

817		PARIS (F), 9 November 1797—August (?) 1798, *review mark for large items*
818		FRANCE, 9 November 1797—August (?) 1798, *general review for small items*
819		PARIS (F), 1809—1819, *guarantee for medium-sized items*
820		BELGIUM, 1831—1869, *"Garantie" — official test of purity*
821		FRANCE, from 1838 up to the present, *guarantee and purity 950/1000 — for large items*
822		FRANCE, from 1838 up to the present, *guarantee and purity 800/1000 — for large items*
823		PARIS (F), 1819—1838, *purity 950/1000*
824		FRANCE — *departments,* 1819—1838, *purity 950/1000*
825		TUNISIA, since 1905, *purity 800/1000 — small items*

826
827

828
829

FORMER AUSTRO-HUNGARIAN EMPIRE, 1 January 1867—1 April 1872, *purity 950/1000, purity 900/1000, purity 800/1000, purity 750/1000; for significance of letter stamped next to mark see marks Nos. 830—833*

830
831

832
833

FORMER AUSTRO-HUNGARIAN EMPIRE, 1 April 1872—1 May 1922 (on the territory of the Austrian Republic), *purity 950/1000, purity 900/1000, purity 800/1000, purity 750/1000*

Key to the Marks:

A — Vienna (A)
B — Linz (A)
C — Prague (CZ)
D — Brno (CZ)
E — Cracow (PL)
F — Lvov (Ukraine)
G — Graz (A)
H — Hall (A) (up to 1872)
H — Bregenz (A) (since 1872)
K — Klagenfurt (A)
L — Ljubljana (Slovenia)
M — Trieste (I)
N — Zadar (Croatia) (only in 1866—67)
P — Pest (H)
R — Košice (SK)
T — Timişoara (R)
U — Alba Iulia (R)
V — Zagreb (Croatia)

834
835
836

HUNGARY, 1937—1965, *for large items: purity 935/1000, purity 900/1000, purity 800/1000*

837

RUSSIA, 1908—1917, *purity 875/1000 (84 zolotniks), for items weighing less than 8.5 g*

838

RUSSIA, 1908—1917, *purity 875/1000 (84 zolotniks), for items weighing more than 8.5 g*

839

RUSSIA, 1908—1917, *imported items*

840

RUSSIA, 1908—1917, *items of sub-standard purity*

841

FORMER U.S.S.R., 1921—1958, *purity 875/1000, for items weighing less than 10 g*

842

FORMER U.S.S.R., 1927—1958, *for items weighing more than 10 g*

843

FORMER U.S.S.R., 1927—1958, *imported items*

844

FORMER U.S.S.R., 1927—1958, *items of sub-standard purity (of historical or artistic value)*

845

FORMER U.S.S.R., 1927—1958, *for decorative or subsidiary parts of the item*

846

BELGIUM, 1831—1869, *mark of purity*

847

LYON (F), 1775—1780,
décharge — large items

848

TOURS (F), 1780—1789,
décharge — minor items

849

PARIS (F), 1 September—31 October, 1809, *review mark for medium-sized items*

850

LYON (F), 1762—1768,
older items

851

LYON (F), 1762—1768,
imported items

852

FRANCE, 1 September—31 October, 1809, *general review mark for small items*

853

PARIS (F), 1781—1789,
contremarque

854

PARIS (F), 1 September—31 October, 1809, *review mark for small items*

855

ORLÉANS (F), 1774—1780,
décharge — large items

856

BOURGES (F), 1774—1780,
décharge — large items

857

BESANÇON (F), 15th century

858

SCHWÄBISCH HALL (D), 18th century

859

NANTES (F), 1762—1769, *imported items*

860

PARIS (F), 1762—1768, *contremarque*

861

ANTWERP (B), 1627—1628

862

ANTWERP (B), 1574—1575

863

ALTENBURG (D), 17th century

864

VOLOGDA (Russia), 1751

865

VOLOGDA (Russia), 1796—1798

866

VOLOGDA (Russia), 1843—1850

867

VALK (Russia), 1785

868		KIROV (Vyatka) (Russia), 18th century
869		SOLIKAMSK (Russia), 1736
870		NITRA (SK), *shield changes shape, sometimes the date is given*
871		ESKILSTUNA (S), 18th century
872		JOENSUU (SF), up to 1943
873		ESKILSTUNA (S), 19th century
874		VORONEZH (Russia), 1852—1869
875		PARIS — GÉNÉRALITÉ (F), (revenue district), 1775—1781, *imported items*
876		RIOM (F), 1774—1780, *décharge — large items*
877		GRENOBLE (F), 1775—1780, *décharge — large items*

878  BAYONNE (F), 1774—1780, *décharge — minor items*

879  TOURS (F), 1774—1780, *décharge — large items*

880  VILNIUS (Vilno) (Lithuania), 1861

881  FILIPSTAD (S), 1st half of 19th century

882 

MOSCOW (Russia), 1741—1775, *different variations*

883 

MOSCOW (Russia), 1780

884  MOSCOW (Russia), 1800—1804

885  POLOTSK (Byelorussia), 1842—1858

886 

TBILISI (Tiflis) (Georgia), 1847—1861

887  SKÄNNINGE (S), 19th century

MAMMALS

888  YSTAD (S), 18th—19th centuries

889  GRAZ (A), 17th century up to 1717

890  SCHWÄBISCH-GMÜND (D), c. 1762—1786

891  KAZAN (Russia), 2nd half of 18th century and 1st half of 19th century

892 

KAZAN (Russia), 1742

893 

KAZAN (Russia), 1880—1890, *numeral indicates purity*

894  FLORENCE (I), 16th(?) century

895  FRANCE — departments, 1838—1879, *import mark for silver watches*

896  KAZAN (Russia), 1864

897  SWEDEN, ÖSTERGÖTLAND PROVINCE, 18th century

898

VENICE (I), 17th—18th centuries

899

VENICE (I), 16th—18th centuries

900

FORMER YUGOSLAVIA, import mark valid from 1882 to 1919 on the territory of the former Serbian Kingdom

901

SCHWÄBISCH-GMÜND (D), early to mid-19th century, *changing shield*

902

BIBERACH a. RISS (D), 18th—19th centuries

903

BIBERACH a. RISS (D), 18th—19th centuries

904

ENGLAND, 1544—1550, *lion passant*

905

ENGLAND, 1550—1558, *lion passant*

906

ENGLAND, 1558—1679, *lion passant*

907

ENGLAND, 1679—1697 and 1719—1739, *lion passant*

908

GREAT BRITAIN, 1739—1756, *lion passant*

909  GREAT BRITAIN, 1756—1822, *lion passant*

910  GREAT BRITAIN, 1822—1896, *lion passant*

911  GREAT BRITAIN, 1822—1896, *lion passant*

912  HEIDELBERG (D), 17th—18th centuries, *various shields*

913  BRUNSWICK (D), 17th—18th centuries, *various shields*

914  DARMSTADT (D), 18th—19th centuries

915  HANOVER-NEUSTADT (D), 17th—18th centuries

916  WEIMAR (D), late 17th century

917  DIJON (F), mid-18th century, *décharge*

918  BAUSKA (Latvia), 18th century

919  PASSAU (D), 18th century

920		INGOLSTADT (D), 18th century
921		LÜNEBURG (D), 16th—17th centuries, *many variations in different shields*
922		ESTONIA, c. 1920—c. 1939
923		BOLOGNA (I), 18th century
924		KALMAR (S), 17th—18th centuries
925		LYON (F), 1762—1768, *décharge — small items*
926		NORWAY, since 1893, *purity 925—830/1000*
927		LUCCA (I), 17th century
928		VITRÉ (F), 1756—1762, *charge*
929 930	 	NETHERLANDS, 1814—1953, *purity 934/1000, purity 833/1000*
931		MORAT (CH), late 18th century

932

VLADIMIR (Russia), 1763—1778

933

VLADIMIR (Russia), 1857—1863

934

VLADIMIR (Russia), 19th century

935

PSKOV (Russia), 19th century

936

DÜSSELDORF (D), 18th century

937

KALMAR (S), end of 18th century and 19th century

938

JÖNKÖPING (S), 18th—19th centuries

939

SAULGAU (D), 1707

940

KARLSHAMN (S), 18th—19th centuries

941

KARLOVY VARY (CZ), 17th—18th centuries

942		ORADEA (R), *shield changes shape, sometimes with date*
943		FLORENCE (I), 17th—18th centuries
944		BRUSSELS (Bruxelles) (B), early 18th century
945		BRUSSELS (Bruxelles) (B), 1750—*c.* 1760
946		LIÈGE (Luik) (B), 1764—1771
947		LIÈGE (Luik) (B), 1784—1792
948		PARMA (I), 17th century
949		PRAGUE (CZ), 1776—1793, *13 lot silver, changing date in the mark*
950		PRAGUE (CZ), 1776—1793, *13 lot silver, changing date in the mark*
951		PRAGUE (CZ), 1793—1806, *13 lot silver, changing date in the mark*

952		PREŠOV (SK), 1st half of 19th century, *changing date and changing shape of the shield*
953		GRAZ (A), 1718—1775
954		GRAZ (A), 1775—1799
955		GRAZ (A), 1800—1806
956		KLAGENFURT (A), 1775—1806
957		NAMUR (Namen) (B), 16th—17th centuries, *sometimes the date changes in the mark*
958		ZWEIBRÜCKEN (D), 18th century
959		RIBE (DK), 18th—19th centuries
960		DÜSSELDORF (D), 18th century
961		SARAGOSSA (E), 16th century

962  YORK (GB), 1700—1857, *several variations*

963  LINKÖPING (S), 18th century

964  LINKÖPING (S), 19th century

965  AMIENS (F), 1762—1774, *décharge — large items*

966  AMIENS (F), 1774—1780, *décharge — large items*

967  ENGLAND, up to c. 1470, *leopard's head*

968  ENGLAND, 1470—1515, *leopard's head, many variations*

969  ENGLAND 16th—17th centuries, *leopard's head, many variations*

970  ENGLAND, 1681—1689, *leopard's head, many variations*

971  GREAT BRITAIN, 1719—1740, *leopard's head, many variations*

972		GREAT BRITAIN, 1756—1821, *leopard's head, many variations*
973		GREAT BRITAIN, 1822—1836, *leopard's head, many variations*
974		GREAT BRITAIN, 1836—1896, *leopard's head, many variations*
975		GREAT BRITAIN, 1710—1711, *lion's head erased*
976		GREAT BRITAIN, 1717—1718, *lion's head erased*
977		GREAT BRITAIN, 1726—1727, *lion's head erased*
978		GREAT BRITAIN, 1725—1731, *lion's head erased*
979		GREAT BRITAIN, 1863—1864, *lion's head erased*
980		BRUGES (B), c. 1660
981		LYON (F), 1780—1791, *décharge — minor items*

982

FORMER AUSTRO-HUNGARIAN EMPIRE, 1 January, 1867—1 April, 1872; *for very small items of 750/1000 purity. For significance of letter stamped next to mark, see marks Nos. 830—833*

983

FORMER AUSTRO-HUNGARIAN EMPIRE, 1 April, 1872—1 May, 1922 (on the territory of the Austrian Republic), *for very small items of 750/1000 purity. For significance of letter in the mark see marks Nos. 830—833*

984

STUTTGART (D), 18th—19th centuries, *sometimes the mark contains a letter*

985

PARIS (F), 1732—1738, *décharge — large and medium-sized items*

986

HANOVER (D), 18th century, *court silversmiths*

987

WOLFENBÜTTEL (D), 17th—18th century

988

DEBRECEN (H), 1st half of 19th century

989

HORSENS (DK), 18th century

990

BRANIEWO (Braunsberg) (PL), c. 1740

991		PERTH (GB), 1679—1710, *several variations*
992		LIMOGES (F), 1780—1791, *décharge — large items*
993		FORMER YUGOSLAVIA, 1919—1933, *imported items, purity 800/1000*
994		FORMER YUGOSLAVIA, 1882—1919, *for small items of 800/1000 purity, valid on the territory of the Serbian Kingdom*
995		PARIS (F), 1794—1797, *guarantee of the goldsmiths' guild for purity 843/1000*(?) *(also import mark up to 1840?)*
996		PARIS (F), 1797, purity 843/1000
997		TOULOUSE (F), 1768—1774, *décharge*
998		LYON (F), 1775—1780, *décharge — minor items*
999		VERSAILLES (F), 1762, *décharge — large items*
1000		CAEN (F), 1780—1791, *décharge — large items*

1001  PAU (F), late 18th century

1002  PAU (F), 1784—1791

1003  FRANCE — Division Centre, 1819—1838, *guarantee for small items*

1004  MARIESTAD (S), 18th—19th centuries

1005  BOURGES (F), 1774—1780 *décharge — minor items*

1006  MARIESTAD (S), 18th century

1007  PARIS (F), 1738—1744, *décharge — large items*

1008  PARIS (F), 1775—1781, *décharge — large items*

1009  LA ROCHELLE (F), 1774—1780, *décharge — small items*

1010  RENNES (F), 1780—1789, *décharge — minor items*

1011

WISMAR (D), from the end of 17th century to the beginning of 19th century, *many variations of the shield*

1012

SWITZERLAND, 1882—1892, *purity 875/1000*

1013
1014

SWITZERLAND, 1893—1934, *purity 875/1000, larger items, smaller items*

1015

BERLIN, 1st half of 18th century

1016

BERLIN, 2nd half of 18th century, *letter in the mark changes*

1017

YAROSLAVL (Russia), 2nd quarter of 18th century

1018

YAROSLAVL (Russia), 2nd half of 18th century

1019

YAROSLAVL (Russia), 1771—1806

1020

MADRID (E), 18th century

1021

BAMBERG (D), 18th—19th centuries

1022		NOVGOROD (Russia), 1764—1846
1023		BERN (CH), 16th century
1024		BERN (CH), 16th century
1025		BERN (CH), 16th century
1026		BERN (CH), c. 1800
1027		NIZHNI NOVGOROD (Russia), 1778—1800
1028		ALINGSÅS (S), late 18th century and early 19th century
1029		PARIS (F), 1768—1774, *items for export*
1030		ROSTOV (Yaroslavski) (Russia), 1761
1031		GIENGEN (D), 18th century
1032		CHUR (CH), 16th—18th centuries

1033		VARBERG (S), 18th—19th centuries
1034		NIZHNI NOVGOROD (Russia), 1859
1035		ST-GERMAIN (F), 1732, *charge*
1036		FORMER FRENCH EAST AFRICA, since 1939, *purity 950/1000; changing letter in the mark*
1037		FORMER FRENCH EAST AFRICA, since 1939, *purity 800/1000; changing letter in the mark*
1038		RHODESIA, present-day mark
1039		NANTES (F), 1746, *décharge*
1040		NANTES (F), 1769—1784, *décharge*
1041		ÖSTERSUND (S), 19th century
1042		COMPIÈGNE (F), 1784—1789

1043  PITEÅ (S), 2nd half of 18th century and 19th century

1044  PARIS (F), 1750—1756, *larger older items*

1045  SAUMUR (F), 1756—1762, *décharge*

1046  UMEÅ (S), 2nd half of 18th century and 19th century

1047  STUTTGART (D), 19th century

1048  ELGAVA (Mitava) (Latvia), 17th century

1049  PARIS (F), 1768—1774, *larger older items*

1050  TUTTLINGEN (D), *c.* 1660

1051  FORMER CZECHOSLOVAKIA, 1921—1928, *purity 750/1000; for smaller items*

1052  FORMER YUGOSLAVIA, 1919—1933, *purity 800/1000; for small items*

1053  CAEN (F), 1780—1791, *décharge, minor items*

1054  TOURS (F), 1753, *décharge*

1055  POITIERS (F), 1774—1780, *décharge, minor items*

1056  SCHAFFHAUSEN (CH), 16th century

1057  SCHAFFHAUSEN (CH), 17th—18th centuries

1058  HUDIKSVALL (S), 18th century

1059  HUDIKSVALL (S), 18th—19th centuries

1060  METZ (F), 1774—1780, *décharge, large items*

1061  AMIENS (F), 1780—1790, *décharge, minor items*

1062  PARIS (F), 1819—1838, *guarantee for smaller items*

1063  ORLÉANS (F), 1774—1780, *décharge, minor items*

1064  FRANCE, general review from 10 May to 1 October, 1838; *for large items*

1065  LYON (F), 1768—1775, *décharge, small items*

1066  PONTOISE (F), 1768—1774, *contremarque*

1067  PARIS (F), *contremarque décharge, large items*

1068  LA ROCHELLE (F), 1780—1791, *décharge, minor items*

1069  PARIS (F), 1775—1781 *décharge, small items*

1070  FORMER CZECHOSLOVAKIA, 1921—1928, *purity 900/1000, for smaller items*

1071  LIMOGES (F), 1780—1781, *décharge, minor items*

1072  MONTARGIS (F), 1768—1774, *décharge*

1073  ROUEN (F), 1698, *décharge*

1074  SALINS (F), 1784—1789

1075  WINTERTHUR (CH), 18th century

1076  SAUMUR (F), 18th century, *charge*

1077  CAEN (F), 1744—1750, *décharge, minor items*

1078		PARIS (F), 1744—1750, *décharge, large items*
1079		CAEN (F), 1744—1750, *décharge, large items*
1080		ST-GERMAIN (F), 1781, *décharge, medium-sized items*
1081		PARIS (F), 1738—1744, *décharge, minor items*
1082		PARIS (F), 1732—1738, *décharge, minor items*
1083		PARIS (F), 1762—1768, *décharge, minor items*
1084		ANGERS (F), 1747, *décharge*
1085		TOURS (F), 1768—1774, *décharge*
1086		FORMER CZECHOSLOVAKIA, 1921—1928, *purity 800/1000, for smaller items*
1087		HUNGARY, 1937—1965, *purity 935/1000, for small items*
1088		HUNGARY, 1937—1965, *purity 800/1000, for small items*
1089		PARIS-GÉNÉRALITÉ (revenue district) (F), 1775—1781, *items for export*

1090 

PARIS-GÉNÉRALITÉ (revenue district) (F), *1775—1781, older items*

1091 

FRANCE, general review from 16 August to 16 November, 1819, *for large items, the numeral in the mark indicates the seat of the Assay Office, here 57—department Nord, Lille*

1092 

FORMER AUSTRO-HUNGARIAN EMPIRE, 1 January, 1867—1 April, 1872, purity 800/1000, *for very small items*

1093 

FORMER AUSTRO-HUNGARIAN EMPIRE, 1 March, 1872—1 May, 1922 (on the territory of the Austrian Republic), *purity 800/1000 for very small items*

1094 

PARIS (F), 1797, *purity 950/1000*

1095 

FRANCE, general review from 10 May to 1 October, 1838, *for very small items*

1096 

POITIERS (F), 1774—1780, *décharge, large items*

1097
1098  

MEAUX (F), 1784—1789

1099 

TOURS (F), 1774—1780, *décharge, minor items*

1100 

ST-GERMAIN, (F) 1732, *décharge*

1101 

LA CHARITÉ (F), 1768—1774, *décharge*

1102 

TROYES (F) 1768—1774, *décharge*

1103 

SWIDNICA (Schweidnitz) (PL), 17th—18th centuries

1104
1105 

LISBON (P), 1886—1938, *purity 916/1000, purity 833/1000, for large items; tolerance 005/1000*

1106
1107 

OPORTO (P), 1886—1938, *purity 916/1000, purity 833/1000; for large items; tolerance 005/1000*

1108
1109 

GONDOMAR (P), 1886—1913, *purity 916/1000, purity 833/1000; for large items; tolerance 005/1000*

1110
1111 

BRAGA (P), 1886—1911, *purity 916/1000, purity 833/1000; for large items; tolerance 005/1000*

1112
1113 

GONDOMAR (P), 1913—1938, *purity 916/1000, purity 833/1000; for large items; tolerance 005/1000*

1114
1115 

LISBON (P), 1886—1938, *purity 916/1000, purity 833/1000; for small items; tolerance 005/1000*

1116
1117 

OPORTO (P), 1886—1938, *purity 916/1000, purity 833/1000; for small items; tolerance 005/1000*

No.	Mark	Description
1118 1119	 	GONDOMAR (P), 1886—1913, *purity 916/1000, purity 833/1000; for small items; tolerance 005/1000*
1120 1121	 	BRAGA (P), 1886—1911, *purity 916/1000; purity 833/1000; for small items; tolerance 005/1000*
1122 1123	 	GONDOMAR (P), 1913—1938, *purity 916/1000, purity 833/1000; for small items; tolerance 005/1000*
1124		FORMER YUGOSLAVIA, 1919—1933, *purity 750/1000, for large items*
1125		PARIS (F), 1750—1756, *décharge, large items*
1126		BORDEAUX (F), 1744—1750, *décharge*
1127		PARIS (F), guarantee since 1838; *for small items*
1128		TOULOUSE (F), 1780—1789, *décharge, large items*
1129		PARIS (F), 1768—1774, *medium-sized older items*
1130		RIOM (F), 1780—1789, *décharge, minor items*

1131 

IRKUTSK (Russia), 1777—1789

1132 
TOBOLSK (Russia), 1765—1780

1133 
IRKUTSK (Russia), 1815—1825

1134 
UFA (Russia), mid-19th century

1135 
KRISTIINA (SF), up to 1943

1136 
PARIS (F), 1697—1703, *décharge, large items*

1137 
WESEL (D), 16th—17th centuries; *sometimes together with date letters*

1138 
LA ROCHELLE (F), 1774—1780, *décharge, large items*

1139 

ST-GERMAIN (F), 1784—1789

1140 

JIHLAVA (CZ), 1769—1806?, *changing date in the mark*

BIRDS

1141 

1142 

PARMA and PIACENZA (I), 1818—1872, *purity 917/1000, purity 792/1000; for smaller items*

1143 

1144 

PARMA and PIACENZA (I), 1818—1872, *purity 917/1000, purity 792/1000*

1145 

DONAUWÖRTH (D), 16th—17th centuries

1146 

LIÈGE (Luik) (B), mid-16th century

1147 

LIÈGE (Luik) (B), 1650—1688

1148 

LIÈGE (Luik) (B), 1688—1693

1149 

LIÈGE (Luik) (B), 1693—1705?

1150 

LIÈGE (Luik) (B), 1693

1151 

LIÈGE (Luik) (B), 1711—1723

1152 

LIÈGE (Luik) (B), 1724—1743

1153 

LIÈGE (Luik) (B), 1744—1763

1154 
LIÈGE (Luik) (B), 1764—1771

1155 

LIÈGE (Luik) (B), 1772—1784

1156 

LIÈGE (Luik) (B), 1784—1792

1157 

NOVGOROD (Russia), 1717—1732

1158 

TULA (Russia), 1794

1159 

VELIKY USTYUG (Russia), 1768—1782

1160 

GALICIA (Ukraine), 1769

1161 

KALUGA (Russia), 1772—1786

1162		KAMENETS-PODOLSK (Ukraine), 1758—1764
1163		MOSCOW (Russia), 1712; *many variations*
1164		MOSCOW (Russia), 1675—1676; *many variations*
1165		MOSCOW (Russia), 1700—1710; *many variations*
1166		MOSCOW (Russia), 1740; *many variations*
1167		MOSCOW (Russia), 1731; *many variations*
1168		LÜBECK (D), 16th—18th centuries; *many variations*
1169		ST PETERSBURG (Russia), 1730—1737; *many variations*
1170		PERTH (GB), up to 1750 (1856?); *various deviations*
1171		MIDDELBURG (NL), 18th century

1172  BOLSWARD (NL), 18th century

1173  TRIESTE (I), 18th century

1174  MINSK (Byelorussia), 1871

1175  ÜBERLINGEN (D), 16th—17th centuries

1176  BRNO (CZ), from mid-17th century to 1768

1177  BRNO (CZ), 1769—1806?; *changing date in the mark*

1178  ZNOJMO (CZ), 1769—1806?; *changing date in the mark*

1179  OLOMOUC (CZ), 1769—1806?; *changing date in the mark*

1180  MECHELEN (B), 18th century

1181
1182   LISBON (P), 1886—1938; *purity 916/1000, purity 833/1000, for large items; tolerance 002/1000*

1183
1184

OPORTO (P), 1886—1938, *purity 916/1000, purity 833/1000, for large items; tolerance 002/1000*

1185
1186

GONDOMAR (P), 1886—1913, *purity 916/1000, purity 833/1000, for large items; tolerance 002/1000*

1187
1188

BRAGA (P), 1886—1911, *purity 916/1000, purity 833/1000, for large items; tolerance 002/1000*

1189
1190

GONDOMAR (P), 1913—1938, *purity 916/1000, purity 833/1000, for large items; tolerance 002/1000*

1191

SCHWEINFURT (D), 17th century; *several variations*

1192

ÜBERLINGEN (D), 18th century

1193

AACHEN (D), from 1573 to the beginning of 19th century; *sometimes with date letter*

1194

FRANKFURT a.M. (D), 16th century — mid-18th century; *different variations in stamps*

1195

U.S.A., Isaiah Wagster, 1776—1793; *Baltimore, Md.*

1196

MODENA (I), 1818—1872, *purity 10 oncie 10/12*

1197  MODENA (I), 1818—1872, *purity 11 oncie 11/12*

1198  MODENA (I), 17th century

1199  TURIN (I), c. 1750

1200  PRUSSIA, tax mark for items manufactured after 25 April, 1809; from 10 September, 1809, onwards for church items exempt from tax (Gratisstempel)

1201  PALERMO (I), 17th century

1202  FRANKFURT a.M. (D), mid-18th century

1203  NEUCHÂTEL (CH), 17th—18th centuries

1204  ARAD (R), early 19th century

1205  ARAD (R), 1847

1206  POTSDAM (D), 18th century

1207 

OLOMOUC (CZ), prior to 1769; *changing date in the mark*

1208 

ARBOGA (S), 17th—18th centuries

1209 

ARBOGA (S), 17th—18th centuries

1210 

ÖREBRO (S), 17th—18th centuries

1211 

CHERNIGOV (Ukraine), 1st half of 19th century

1212 

MEMMINGEN (D), 16th—17th centuries; *different variations in shields*

1213 

RACIBÓRZ (Ratibor) (PL), 17th century

1214 

BYTOM (PL), 1736—1770

1215 

KAUFBEUREN (D), 18th century

1216 

GENEVA (CH), 18th century

1217		PREŠOV (SK), 18th century
1218		WERTHEIM (D), c. 1660
1219		HILDESHEIM (D), 16th—17th centuries
1220		CHEB (CZ), 17th—18th centuries
1221		ORENBURG (Russia), mid-19th century
1222		SUZDAL (Russia), mid-18th century
1223		PARIS (F), 1713—1717, *décharge*
1224		FRANCE, 1798—1809, *purity 950/1000*
1225		FRANCE, 1798—1809, *purity 800/1000*
1226		PARIS (F), 1809—1819, *purity 950/1000*

1227  PARIS (F), 1809—1819, *purity 800/1000*

1228  FRANCE — departments, 1809—1819, *purity 950/1000*

1229  FRANCE — departments, 1809—1819, *purity 800/1000*

1230
1231
1232

FORMER YUGOSLAVIA, since 1933, *purity 950/1000, purity 900/1000, purity 800/1000, for small items*

1233  TONGEREN (Tongres) (B), c. 1759

1234  ZWICKAU (D), 16th—17th centuries

1235
1236
1237

PARIS (F), 1727—1732, *décharge, medium-sized items*

1238  PAU (F), mid-18th century

1239  TOULOUSE (F), 1755, *décharge*

1240  's GRAVENHAGE (NL), 18th century

1241  ROUEN (F), 1768—1774, *décharge*

1242  TOULOUSE (F), 1774—1780, *décharge, minor items*

1243  TOURS (F), late 17th century, *décharge*

1244  PARIS-GÉNÉRALITÉ (revenue district) (F), 1756—1762, *décharge, large items*

1245  BEAUVAIS (F), 1768—1774, *décharge*

1246  KÄKISALMI (SF), up to 1943

1247  PARIS (F), 1704—1712, *contremarque, minor items*

1248  PARIS (F), 1722—1727, *décharge, minor items*

1249  EINSIEDELN (CH), 17th—18th centuries

1250  EINSIEDELN (CH), 18th century

1251  CHARTRES (F), 1784—1789

1252  FORMER YUGOSLAVIA, since 1933, *import mark for purity 800/1000*

1253  OPORTO (P), 1886—1938, *special items*

1254  LISBON (P), 1886—1938, *special items*

1255  BRAGA (P), 1886—1911, GONDOMAR (P), 1913—1938, *special items*

1256  VERSAILLES (F), 1768—1774, *décharge, large items*

1257  PARIS-GÉNÉRALITÉ (revenue district) (F), 1756—1762, *décharge, large items*

1258  GRENOBLE (F), 1770, *contremarque*

1259  PARIS-GÉNÉRALITÉ (revenue district) (F), 1768—1774, *décharge, large items*

1260  TOULOUSE (F), 1762—1768, *décharge*

1261  FALKENBERG (S), 18th—19th centuries

1262  FRANKFURT a.d.ODER (D), 17th—18th centuries

1263
1264

SWITZERLAND, 1893—1934, *purity 800/1000; larger items, smaller items*

1265

SWITZERLAND, 1882—1892, *purity 800/1000*

1266
1267

LISBON (P), 1886—1938, *purity 916/1000, purity 833/1000, for small items; tolerance 002/1000*

1268
1269

OPORTO (P), 1886—1938, *purity 916/1000, purity 833/1000, for small items; tolerance 002/1000*

1270
1271

GONDOMAR (P), 1886—1913, *purity 916/1000, purity 833/1000, for small items; tolerance 002/1000*

1272
1273

BRAGA (P), 1886—1911, *purity 916/1000, purity 833/1000, tolerance 002/10000*

1274
1275

GONDOMAR (P), 1913—1938, *purity 916/1000, purity 833/1000, for small items; tolerance 002/1000*

1276

FRANCE, general review from 1 September to 31 October, 1809; *for medium-sized items*

1277

PARIS (F), 1781—1789, *imported items*

1278

PARIS (F), 1783, *décharge, medium-sized items*

1279

PARIS (F), 1798, *purity 800/1000*

1280
1281

PARIS (F), 1798, *purity 950/1000, purity 900/1000*

1282

TOULOUSE (F), *décharge, minor items*

1283

PARIS (F), 1744—1750, *décharge, minor items*

1284

PARIS (F), 1783, *décharge, small items*

1285

FORMER YUGOSLAVIA, 1882—1919, *purity 750/1000, for small items; valid on the territory of the former Serbian Kingdom*

1286

GRENOBLE (F), 1770, *contremarque*

1287

PARIS-GÉNÉRALITÉ (revenue district) (F), 1768—1774, *décharge, minor items*

1288

PARIS (F), 1750—1766, *décharge, small items*

1289

SAUMUR (F), 1756—1762, *charge*

1290

HUNGARY, 1937—1965, *purity 900/1000, small items*

1291

MALMÖ (S), 17th—19th centuries

1292

MALMÖ (S), 17th—19th centuries

1293		SZCZECIN (Stettin) (PL), 18th century
1294		BEAUMONT-SUR-OISE (F), 1768—1774, *décharge*
1295		FREIBURG i.B. (D), 17th—18th centuries
1296		PARIS (F), 1717—1722, *contremarque, large items*
1297		CHÂTEAU GONTIER (F), 18th century
1298		FORMER YUGOSLAVIA, 1919—1933, *purity 750/1000, small items*
1299		CHARTRES (F), 1768—1774, *décharge*
1300		LYON (F), 1768—1755, *contremarque*
1301		ETAMPES (F), 1768—1774, *contremarque*
1302		PONTOISE (F), 1768—1774, *décharge*

OTHER ANIMALS

1303

FRANCE — DIVISION NORD-EST, 1819—1838, *guarantee for small items*

1304

FRANCE — DIVISION SUD-OUEST, 1819—1838, *guarantee for small items*

1305

PARIS (F), 1738—1744, *contremarque*

1306

MELUN (F), 1784—1789

1307

LAHOLM (S), 18th—19th centuries

1308

MARSTRAND (S), 18th—19th centuries

1309

ÖSTHAMMAR (S), 18th—19th centuries

1310

SIMRISHAMN (S), 19th century

1311

NARVA (Russia), 17th century

1312  NARVA (Russia), 18th century

1313  ENGELHOLM (S), 18th—19th centuries

1314  UUSIKAUPUNKI (SF), up to 1943

1315  SARATOV (Russia), 2nd half of 18th century—19th century

1316  ENKHUISEN (NL), 18th century

1317
1318
1319

ROMANIA, 1906—1920?,
purity 950/1000,
purity 800/1000,
purity 750/1000

1320  FRANCE — DIVISION SUD, 1819—1938, *guarantee for small items*

1321  FRANCE — DIVISION NORD-OUEST, 1819—1838, *guarantee for small items*

1322  BEAUVAIS (F), 1784—1789, *décharge*

1323  TOURS (F), early 18th century, *décharge*

1324  SIMRISHAMN (S), 18th century

1325  ST-GERMAIN (F), 1756, *décharge*

1326  PARIS (F), 1744—1750, *older large items*

1327  RENNES (F), 1740, *charge*

1328  NANTES (F), 1731, *décharge*

1329  PARIS (F), 1783, *contremarque*

1330  BRAY-SUR-SEINE (F), 1768—1774, *décharge*

1331  TOULOUSE (F), 17th century, *décharge*

1332  LYON (F), 1768—1775, *imported items*

1333  PARIS (F), 1756—1762, *décharge, minor items*

1334  BORDEAUX (F), 1780—1789, *décharge, minor items*

1335 

FRANCE — DIVISION EST, 1819—1838, *guarantee for small items*

1336 

PARIS (F), 1768—1774, *import mark for small items*

1337 

PROVINS (F), 1768—1774, *décharge*

1338 

ETAMPES (F), 1784—1789

1339 

FRANCE, 1838—1893, *guarantee for silver watches*

1340 

FRANCE, 1838 up to the present, *"petit" guarantee for small items*

1341 

LYON (F), 1768—1775, *décharge, large items*

1342 

PARIS (F), 1762—1768, *décharge, large items*

1343 

FRANCE — DIVISION OUEST, 1819—1838, *guarantee for small items*

1344 

ROUEN (F), 1768—1774, *décharge*

1345 

ETAMPES (F), 1768—1774, *décharge*

1346  FRANCE, 1838—1864, *import mark*

1347  LISBON (P), since 1891, *for watches of 800/1000 purity*

1348  OPORTO (P), since 1891, *for watches of 800/1000 purity*

1349  LISBON (P), since 1891, *plaqué*

1350  OPORTO (P), since 1891, *plaqué*

1351  FRANCE — DIVISION SUD-EST, 1819—1838, *guarantee for small items*

1352  FONTAINEBLEAU (F), 1768—1774, *contremarque*

1353  FORMER CZECHOSLOVAKIA, 1921, *inventory mark*

1354  COULOMMIERS (F), 1768—1774, *contremarque*

1355  GIEN (F), 1768—1774, *décharge*

1356  COMPIÈGNE (F), 1768—1774, *décharge*

1357		METZ (F), 1780—1791, *décharge, small items*
1358		PARIS (F), 1722—1727, *contremarque*
1359		FRANCE — DIVISION NORD, 1819—1838, *guarantee for small items*
		PLANTS
1360		EKSJÖ (S), 18th—19th centuries
1361		VIMMERBY (S), 18th—19th centuries
1362		STAVANGER (N), 1st half of 18th century
1363		LINDESBERG (S), 18th century
1364		HEDEMORA (S), late 18th century and 19th century
1365		SWEDEN, BLENKINGEN PROVINCE, 18th century
1366		SWEDEN, BLENKINGEN PROVINCE, 18th century

1367  GLASGOW (GB), from 17th century up to the present, *several variations; rectangular stamp since 1781*

1368  sHERTOGENBOSCH (NL), 17th century

1369  TRIESTE (I), 1797—1806, *for 15 lot silver*

1370  TRIESTE (I), 1797—1806, *for 13 lot silver*

1371  HOLBAEK (DK), 19th century

1372  UDDEVALLA (S), 18th—19th centuries

1373  PENZA (Russia), 1854

1374  NORA (S), late 18th century and 19th century

1375  NORA (S), 18th century

1376  FRANCE-departments, 1819—1838, *import mark for small items*

1377		PERONNE (F), 1768—1774, *imported items*
1378		TOULOUSE (F), 1774—1780, *décharge*
1379		TROYES (F), 1780—1789
1380		PARIS (F), 1756—1762, *contremarque*
1381		PARIS (F), 1762—1768, *charge, minor items*
1382		PARIS (F), 1704—1712, *reconnaissance, minor items*
1383		SENS (F), 1768—1774, *contremarque*
1384		VERSAILLES (F), 1768—1774, *charge, medium-sized items*
1385		RIOM (F), 1780—1789, *décharge, large items*
1386		LYON (F), 1762—1768, *older items*

1387  ROUEN (F), 1780—1789, *décharge, large items*

1388  MANTES (F), 1774—1780, *contremarque*

1389  DIJON (F), 1780—1791, *décharge, large items*

1390
1391   TUNISIA, since 1905, *purity 900/1000, purity 800/1000, large items*

1392  ITALY, 1810—1872, *purity 950/1000, for small items*

1393  ST-GERMAIN (F), 1781, *décharge, large items*

1394  PARIS-GÉNÉRALITÉ (revenue district) (F), 1775—1781, *for very small items*

1395  ROUEN (F), 1774—1780, *décharge, minor items*

1396  DIJON (F), 1775—1780, *décharge, large items*

1397  AMIENS (F), 1780—1791, *décharge, large items*

1398		AUGSBURG (D), 1675—1685
1399		AUGSBURG (D), 1680—1696
1400		AUGSBURG (D), 1712—1713
1401		AUGSBURG (D), 1723—1735
1402		AUGSBURG (D), 1723—1735
1403		AUGSBURG (D), *changing letters indicate different periods, here 1787—1789*
1404		RAPPERSWIL (CH), 16th—17th centuries
1405		RAPPERSWIL (CH), 18th century
1406		LANDSKRONA (S), 17th—18th centuries
1407		LANDSKRONA (S), 19th century

1408  FALUN (S), 18th—19th centuries

1409  BORDEAUX (F), late 18th century, *décharge*

1410  VERSAILLES (F), 1780—1789, *décharge, large items*

1411  PARIS (F), review from 16 August to 16 November, 1819; *for large items*

1412  MANTES (F), 1774—1780, *décharge*

1413  GRENOBLE (F), 1780—1791, *décharge, minor items*

1414  SWEDEN, BLENKINGEN PROVINCE, 18th century

1415 

PROVINS (F), 1784—1789

1416  FRANCE-departments, 1819—1838, import mark for large items

1417  MELUN (F), 1774—1780, *décharge*

1418

PARIS (F), 1768—1774,
charge, small items

1419

PARIS (F), 1717—1722,
reconnaissance

1420

LYON (F), 1768—1775,
older items

1421

DREUX (F), 1768—1774,
décharge

1422

LYON (F), 1780—1791,
décharge, large items

1423

BAYONNE (F), 1780—1789,
décharge, minor items

1424

DORDRECHT (NL), 18th century

1425

PARIS (F), 1781—1789,
very small items

1426

PARIS (F), review from 16 August to 16 November, 1819; *for very small items*

1427

ROSENHEIM (D),
mid-17th century

1428		TOULOUSE (F), 16th—17th centuries, *décharge*
1429		NORWICH (GB), 1581—1697; *several variations*
1430		PARIS (F), 1756—1762, *reconnaissance*
1431		BAYONNE (F), 1780—1789, *décharge, large items*
1432		BORDEAUX (F), late 18th century, *décharge*
1433		BORDEAUX (F), late 18th century, *décharge*
1434		LYON (F), 1768—1775, *older items*
1435		BORDEAUX (F), late 18th century, *décharge*
1436		GRENOBLE (F), 1780—1791, *décharge, large items*
1437		ST-GERMAIN (F), 1768—1774, *charge, minor items*

1438  TRONDHEIM (N), changing date in the mark

1439  HANOVER-ALTSTADT (D), 17th—18th centuries; in 17th century two numerals in the mark indicating year

1440  PARIS (F), 1704—1712, *reconnaissance, large items*

1441  BRAŞOV (R), mid-18th century

1442  PARIS (F), 1783, *décharge, very small items*

1443  KIEL (D), 18th century

1444  KIEL (D), 17th century; *changing shield*

1445  PARMA and PIACENZA (I), 1818—1872, *very small items*

1446  PARIS (F), 1684—1687, *very small items*

1447  DIJON (F), 1762—1768, *décharge*

1448		NYSA(Neisse) (PL), 17th—18th centuries; *several varieties of shields; sometimes the mark contains the date*
1449		KOŠICE, (SK), from 16th century to c. 1812
1450		ODENSE (DK), 18th century
1451		JÖNKÖPING (S), 17th—18th centuries
1452		ENKÖPING (S), 18th—19th centuries
1453		DILLINGEN a.d. DONAU (D), 1st half of 18th century
1454		PARIS (F), 1680—1684, *décharge, small items*
1455		GRÄNNA (S), 18th—19th centuries
1456		PARIS (F), 1717—1722, *décharge, large items*
1457		ANGERS (F), 1734—1741, *décharge*

1458  PARIS (F), 1717—1722, *décharge, medium-sized items*

1459  LILLE (F), 1750

1460  LILLE (F), 1755

1461  LILLE (F), 1776

1462  LILLE (F), 1732

1463  PARIS (F), 1717—1722, *contremarque, small items*

1464  PARIS (F), 1717—1722, *décharge, large items*

1465  TOULOUSE (F), 16th—17th centuries, *décharge*

1466  TOULOUSE (F), 1726, *décharge*

1467  TOULOUSE (F), 1768—1774, *décharge*

1468		VERSAILLES (F), 1784
1469		FORMER CZECHOSLOVAKIA, 1921—1940, *imported items*
1470		PARIS (F), 1677—1680, *charge, large items*
1471		PARIS (F), 1680—1684, *charge; this mark was added to other marks in 1681*
1472		PARIS (F), 1727—1732, *décharge, large items*
1473		YORK (GB), 1562—1700; *several variations*
1474		LINCOLN (GB), c. 1624 and during the period 1640—1650
1475		HALMSTAD (S), 18th—19th centuries
1476		GRENOBLE (F), 1768—1774, *imported items*
1477		RENNES (F), 1774—1780, *décharge, large items*

1478  FALUN (S), 18th—19th centuries

1479  KHARKOV (Ukraine), mid-19th century

1480  GŁOGÓWEK (Ober-Glogau) (PL), 18th century

1481  LYON (F), 1762—1768, *imported items*

1482  VERSAILLES (F), 1780—1789, *décharge, medium-sized items*

CELESTIAL BODIES

1483  PARIS (F), 1722—1727, *décharge, large items*

1484  KUOPIO (SF), up to 1943

1485  FÜRTH (D), 19th century

1486  VARKAUS (SF), up to 1943

1487  FORMER YUGOSLAVIA, 1919—1933, *purity 900/1000; larger items*

1488	 	TURKEY, 1939—1942, *purity 900/1000*
1489	 	TURKEY, 1939—1942, *purity 800/1000*
1490		TURKEY, 1923—1928, *purity 900/1000*
1491		TURKEY, 1923—1928, *purity 800/1000*
1492	 	LÜNEBURG (D), since the beginning of 19th century
1493	 	FORMER AUSTRO-HUNGARIAN EMPIRE, 1806—1809, *restamped hallmark for larger items; for significance of letter in the mark see mark No. 84; here indicating Prague*
1494	 	FÜRTH (D), 18th century
1495		GERMANY, since 1888, *minimum purity 800/1000*
1496		HALLE a. d. SAALE (D), 17th—18th centuries; *changing shields*
1497		MAASTRICHT (NL), 18th century

1498  TUNISIA, 1856—1905, *Public Assayer's mark*

1499  PARIS (F), 1684—1687, *reconnaissance*

1500  SPAIN, since 1934, *purity 915/1000*

1501  ROUEN (F), 1768—1774, *décharge*

1502  SPAIN, since 1934, *purity 750/1000*

1503  BRAGA (P), 1881—1887, *minimum purity 750/1000*

1504  GUIMARÃES (P), 1881—1887, *minimum purity 750/1000*

1505  NORDEN (D), 19th century

1506  NORDEN (D), 18th—19th centuries

1507  BOLZANO (I), 18th century

1508		BOLZANO (I), mid-18th century
1509		BOLZANO (I), early 18th century
1510		THUN (CH), 17th century
1511		SION (CH), 17th century
1512		SION (CH), 18th century
1513		DOKKUM (NL), 18th century
1514		HAARLEM (NL), 18th century
1515		GOUDA (NL), 17th century
1516		SÖDERKÖPING (S), 18th—19th centuries
1517		ITALY, 1810—1872, *purity 800/1000, for large items*

ARCHITECTURE

1518  ÅMÅL (S), 18th—19th centuries

1519  LEUTKIRCH (D), 17th century

1520  NYKÖPING (S), 17th—19th centuries; *many variations*

1521  EDINBURGH (GB), 16th—17th centuries; *many variations*

1522  SPEIER (D), 17th century

1523  BERGEN (N), 18th—19th centuries; *changing shields*

1524  ST-GERMAIN (F), 1768—1774, *contremarque*

1525  TOULOUSE (F), 1750—1756, *charge*

1526  TOURS (F), 1780—1789, *décharge, large items*

1527  ORLÉANS (F), 1762, *décharge*

1528

ALKMAAR (NL), 18th century

1529

NORWICH (GB), *1565—1697; several variations*

1530

TOROPETS (Russia), 1802

1531

HANKO (SF), up to 1943

1532

KÖSZEG (H), 1st half of 19th century

1533

BUDAPEST-PEST (H), up to the end of 18th century

1534

BUDAPEST-PEST (H), from c. 1810 to 1865; *changing date*

1535

TIMIŞOARA (R), in different shields and with changing date

1536

NOYON (F), 1768—1774

1537

PRAGUE-NOVÉ MĚSTO (CZ), 1562—1776; *changing date*

1538

MAGDEBURG (D), 17th century and early 18th century; *more variations*

1539

UHERSKÉ HRADIŠTĚ (CZ), early 17th century

1540

RIGA (Latvia), 19th century

1541

NEWCASTLE (GB), since 1672

1542

DENMARK, since 1893; *control mark, minimum standard purity 830/1000*

1543

HÄLSINGBORG (S), 19th century

1544

NOVI SAD (Serbia), since the end of 18th century

1545

FALKÖPING (S), 18th—19th centuries

1546

HÄLSINGBORG (S), 1st half of 18th century

1547

EXETER (GB), 1701 — 2nd half of 19th century; *various deviations*

1548  LUND (S), 18th—19th centuries

1549  LUND (S), 18th century

1550  AALBORG (DK), *sometimes with date in the mark*

1551  HÄLSINGBORG (S), late 18th century

1552  NYKÖPING (S), 17th—19th centuries; *many variations*

1553  ZHITOMIR (Ukraine), 1823

1554  MALBORK(Marienburg) (PL), 17th—18th centuries

1555  SOPRON (H), up to 1780s

1556  JÖNKÖPING (S), 18th—19th centuries

1557  BRATISLAVA (SK), up to 1730s

1558 

ZABKÓWICE
ŚLĄSKIE (Frankenstein) (PL),
early 18th century

1559 

GENOA (I), 17th—18th
centuries

1560 

TOURNAI (Doornijk) (B), 1st
half of 17th century

1561 

BAUTZEN (D), 18th
century

1562 

PRAGUE-STARÉ MĚSTO
(CZ), 1562—1776;
changing date

1563 

BOLESŁAWIEC(Bunzlau)
(PL), c. 1750

1564 

CRACOW (PL), 1809—1835

1565 

ALTONA (D), 18th century;
*changing date letters in the
mark*

1566 

HAMBURG (D), 17th—18th
centuries; *from mid-17th
century onwards date letters
change in the mark*

1567 

KOMÁRNO (SK)
KOMÁROM (H),
1st half of 19th century

1568  BUDAPEST-BUDA (H), up to the end of 18th century

1569  WEILHEIM (D), 17th—18th centuries

1570  COPENHAGEN (DK), since 1608; *changing date in the mark*

1571  BRATISLAVA (SK), from 1730s to 1860s

1572  SOPRON (H), up to mid-19th century; *changing date*

1573  BUDAPEST-BUDA (H), from c. 1810 to 1865; *changing date*

1574  LEÓN (E), 18th century

1575  CRACOW (PL), 1835—1866, *changing date, here 1845*

1576  SKARA (S), 18th—19th centuries

1577  KALUNDBORG (DK), 17th century

1578 

PRAGUE-MALÁ STRANA (CZ), 1666—1776; *changing date in the mark*

1579 

ESZTERGOM (H), early 19th century

1580 
OREL (Russia), 1766

1581 
CORK (Corcaigh) (EIR), 17th—18th centuries; *different varieties*

1582 
KUNGÄLV (S), late 18th century

1583 
KLAIPEDA (Memel) (Lithuania), 18th century

1584 
CRACOW (PL), 1809—1835

1585 

CLUJ (R), from late 18th century to mid-19th century

1586 

BANSKÁ ŠTIAVNICA (SK), 1st half of 19th century

1587 

ALBA IULIA (R), c. 1850

1588 
UHERSKÉ HRADIŠTĚ (CZ), 1769—1806?; *changing date*

1589 
FRIBOURG (CH), c. 1630

1590 
FRIBOURG (CH), c. 1710

1591 
MIKULOV (CZ), 1769—1806?; *changing date*

OBJECTS

1592 
PARIS (F), 1677—1680, *charge, large items*

1593 
PARIS (F), 1691—1698, *décharge*

1594 
STOCKHOLM (S), 1500—1600

1595 
STOCKHOLM (S), 1500—1600

1596 
BRAŞOV (R), mid-19th century

1597 
FINLAND, since 1810, *control mark for domestic items*

1598 

FINLAND, since 1810, *control mark for imported items*

1599
1600
1601 

ROMANIA, 1937—1949; *purity 950/1000, purity 800/1000, purity 750/1000*

1602
1603
1604 

ROMANIA, up to 1937; *purity 950/1000, purity 800/1000, purity 750/1000*

1605 

PARIS (F), 1775—1781; *duty-free items*

1606 

PARIS (F), 1697—1703, *décharge, large items*

1607 

PARIS (F), 1687—1691, *décharge, large items*

1608 

PARIS (F), 1680—1684, *extra mark added in 1681*

1609 

PARIS (F), 1680—1684, *décharge, large items*

1610 

PARIS (F), 1677—1680, *charge, large items*

1611 

BORDEAUX (F), 1687—1691, *décharge*

1612 

SIGTUNA (S), 18th century

1613 

FORMER YUGOSLAVIA, 1919—1933, *imported items of 750/1000 purity*

1614 

PARIS (F), 1768—1774, *duty-free items*

1615 

SHEFFIELD (GB), from 1773 up to the present; *several variations*

1616
1617  

PARIS (F), 1684—1687, *décharge*

1618 

BORDEAUX (F), 1774—1780, *décharge*

1619 

FRANCE, 1809—1819, *import mark for large items*

1620 

OPORTO (P), 1886—1911, *silver rods*

1621 

BRAGA (P), 1886—1911, *silver rods*

1622 

KALININ (Tver) (Russia), 1816—1830

1623 

KALININ (Tver) (Russia), 19th century; *changing date*

1624		KALUGA (Russia), 1864
1625		KALUGA (Russia), 1870—1880
1626		KOBLENZ (D), 18th century
1627		SWEDEN, state control mark used from 1752 up to the present
1628		HULL (GB), 1621—1706
1629		BAKU (Azerbaijan), last quarter of 19th century; *the numeral in the mark indicates purity*
1630		SENLIS (F), 1768—1774, *décharge, medium-sized items*
1631		ELLWANGEN a.d. JAGST (D), 18th century
1632		GHENT (B), 18th century
1633		PARIS (F), 1744—1750, *small older items*

1634		TOURS (F), 18th century, *décharge?*
1635		LANDSHUT (D), mid-18th century
1636		LANDSHUT (D), late 18th century
1637		GRENOBLE (F), 1775—1780, *décharge, minor items*
1638		LA ROCHELLE (F), 1780—1791, *décharge, large items*
1639		PARIS (F), 1768—1774, *imported large items*
1640		PARIS (F), 1781—1789, *Mont de Piété*
1641		MELUN (F), 1774—1780, *contremarque*
1642		DIJON (F), 1774—1780, *décharge, minor items*
1643		LIMOGES (F), 1774—1780, *décharge, minor items*
1644		RIOM (F), 1774—1780, *décharge, small items*

1645 

BOURGES (F), 1780—1789, *décharge, minor items*

1646 

LYON (F), 1768—1775, *imported items*

1647 

VERSAILLES (F), 1762, *décharge, minor items*

1648 

AUDENARDE (Oudenaarde) (B), c. 1600

1649 

AUDENARDE (Oudenaarde) (B), since 1655

1650 

MONTEREAU (F), 1768—1774, *décharge*

1651 

RENNES (F), 1774—1780, *décharge, minor items*

1652 

VESOUL (F), 1784—1789

1653 

BEAUVAIS (F), 1768—1774

1654 

ROUEN (F), 1768—1774, *décharge*

1655 

METZ (F), 1780—1791, *décharge, large items*

1656  ABBEVILLE (F), 1768—1774

1657  PARIS-GÉNÉRALITÉ (revenue district) (F), 1775—1781, *contremarque*

1658  BASEL (CH), mid-17th century

1659  BASEL (CH), 18th century

1660  BASEL (CH), 17th—18th centuries

1661  BASEL (CH), 18th century

1662  NIVELLES (B), 17th century

1663  EGER (H), 1st half of 19th century

1664  LUDWIGSBURG (D), 19th century

1665
1666   ITALY, since 1935, *purity 925/1000*, purity *800/1000*

1667  JAPAN, since 1928; *always with a mark of purity in thousandths*

1668  BELGIUM, 1831—1869, *guarantee for official test of purity*

1669  ESSEN (D), 17th century

1670  ASTRAKHAN (Russia), 2nd half of 18th century

1671  ASTRAKHAN (Russia), 1st half of 19th century

1672  KEŽMAROK (SK), from early 18th century to c. 1800

1673 

KEŽMAROK (SK), c. 1850

1674  HEINOLA (SF), up to 1943

1675 

FREIBERG (D), 18th—19th centuries

1676 

LEIPZIG (D),17th—18th centuries; *changing shields*

1677 

DREṢDEN (D), late 18th century and 19th century

1678 

SIBIU (R), since the end of 18th century

1679 

TOBOLSK (Russia), 1792—1794

1680 

ST-GERMAIN (F), 1768—1774, *décharge, minor items*

1681 

SENLIS (F), 1768—1774, *contremarque*

1682 

FRANCE, 1798—1809, *"poinçon de vieux" for older items put on sale again*

1683 

FRANCE-departments, 1809—1819, *"petite garantie"*

1684 

PARIS (F), 1809—1819, *guarantee for small items*

1685 

FRANCE, 1798—1809, *guarantee for small items*

1686 

PARIS (F), 1722—1727, *décharge, medium-sized items*

1687		ST-GERMAIN (F), 1768—1774, *décharge, large items*
1688		BORDEAUX (F), 1780—1789, *décharge, large items*
1689		SENS (F), 1784—1789
1690		FORMER YUGOSLAVIA, 1919—1933, *purity 900/1000; for small items*
1691	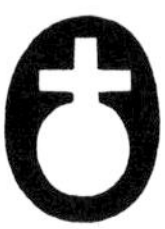	UPPSALA (S), 17th—19th centuries
1692		UPPSALA (S), 17th—19th centuries
1693		SÄTER (S), 19th century
1694		JÁCHYMOV (CZ), 17th—18th centuries
1695		BANSKÁ ŠTIAVNICA (SK), 17th—18th centuries
1696		SALA (S), 17th—19th centuries

1697		FORMER YUGOSLAVIA, 1919—1933, *purity 800/1000, for large items*
1698		BIEL (Bienne) (CH), 18th century
1699		SENLIS (F), 1768—1774, *charge, large items*
1700		BARDEJOV (SK), 18th century
1701		SPIŠSKÁ NOVÁ VES (SK), c. mid-19th century
1702		SORTAVALA (SF), up to 1943
1703		SUNDSVALL (S), 18th—19th centuries
1704		LULEÅ (S), 18th century
1705		LEUVEN (Louvain) (B), 18th century
1706		COULOMMIERS (F), 1768—1774, *décharge*

1707  PÄRNU (Estonia), 18th century

1708  BREMEN (D), 1st half of 18th century

1709  WORMS (D), turn of 17th and 18th century

1710  BREMEN (D), c. 1750

1711  STANS (CH), 18th century

1712  PLZEŇ (Pilsen) (CZ), 18th century

1713  LEGNICA (Liegnitz) (PL), 17th—18th centuries

1714  NEUVILLE (CH), 17th century

1715  RIGA (Latvia), 16th—18th centuries

1716  LEIDEN (NL), 18th century

1717		REGENSBURG (D), 18th century; *without letter G in 16th and 17th centuries*
1718		LULEÅ (S), 19th century
1719		ROME (I), 17th—18th centuries
1720		ROME (I), late 17th century
1721		ROME (I), late 17th century
1722		STADTAMHOF (D), 1767
1723		TARTU (Derpt) (Estonia) 17th—18th centuries
1724		NAUMBURG a.d. SAALE (D), 16th—18th centuries; *many variations in shields*
1725		STRÄNGNÄS (S), 18th—19th centuries
1726		VERSAILLES (F), 1768—1774, *décharge, medium-sized items*

1727

SENLIS (F), 1768—1774,
décharge, large items

1728

MEAUX (F) 1774—1780,
contremarque

1729

BOURGES (F), 1780—1789,
décharge, large items

1730

PARIS (F), 1727—1732,
contremarque

1731

DUBLIN (Baile Átha Cliath) (EIR), 17th—19th centuries;
many variations

1732

PARIS (F), 1781—1789,
older items

1733

BELGIUM, 1831—1869,
state mark of purity

1734

PROVINS (F), 1768—1774,
contremarque

1735

PARIS (F), 1768—1774,
contremarque

1736

URACH (D), c. 1700

1737		HOORN (NL), 17th—18th centuries
1738		STRAUBING (D), mid-18th century
1739		VERSAILLES (F), 1768—1774, *imported items*
1740		SMOLENSK (Russia), 2nd half of 18th century and 19th century
1741		MAINZ (D), 18th century; *date stamped separately*
1742		KULDIGA (Latvia), 18th—19th centuries
1743		OSNABRÜCK (D), early 18th century; *several varieties*
1744		MAINZ (D), 1765—1769
1745		TRNAVA (SK), *shield changes shape; sometimes the mark contains the date*
1746		VÄ (S), 16th century

1747  KREMNICA (SK), up to the end of 18th century

1748  KREMNICA (SK), 1st half of 19th century

1749  MAINZ (D), 19th century

1750  ROYE (F), 1768—1774

1751  ROUEN (F), 1768—1774, *décharge*

1752  MONTDIDIER (F), 1768—1774

1753  MONTREUIL (F), 1768—1774

1754  ROUEN (F), 1774—1780, *décharge, large items*

1755  PERONNE (F), 1768—1774

1756  CALAIS (F), 1768—1774, *imported items*

1757

DIJON (F), 1762—1768, *décharge*

1758

LYON (F), 1762—1768, *contremarque*

1759

LIMOGES (F), 1774—1780, *décharge, large items*

1760

VLISSINGEN (NL), 18th century

1761

DUNDEE (GB), 1628—1840, *many variations*

1762

RENNES (F), 1780—1789, *décharge, large items*

1763

PARIS (F), 1781—1789, *export items*

1764

POITIERS (F), 1780—1791, *décharge, large items*

1765

ST-QUENTIN (F), 1768—1774

1766

ROUEN (F), 1768—1774, *décharge*

1767		NANTES (F), 1762—1769, *décharge*
1768		UUSIKAARLEPYY (SF), up to 1943
1769		DREUX (F), 1768—1774, *contremarque*
1770		BAYONNE (F), 1774—1780, *décharge, large items*
1771		BORÅS (S), 18th—19th centuries
1772		SCHÄRDING (A), *c.* 1600
1773		LONS-LE-SAUNIER (F), 1784—1789
1774		AUXERRE (F), 1784—1789
1775		BESANÇON (F), 1784—1789
1776		EDINBURGH (GB), from 1760 up to the present; *assayer's mark*
1777		BESANÇON (F), 1784—1789

1778		FONTAINEBLEAU (F), 1768—1774, *décharge*
1779		TROYES (F), 1780—1789
1780		BEAUMONT-SUR-OISE (F), 1768—1774, *contremarque*
1781		CAEN (F), 1774—1780, *décharge, minor items*
1782		PARIS-GÉNÉRALITÉ (revenue district) (F), 1775—1781, *reconnaissance*
1783		CAEN (F), 1744—1750, *décharge, minor items*
1784		VERSAILLES (F), 1768—1774, *contremarque*
1785		VERSAILLES (F), 1745, *charge*
1786		AMIENS (F), 1768—1774, *décharge*
1787		PARIS (F), 1781—1789, *reconnaissance*

1788  PARIS (F), 1732—1738, *contremarque*

1789  PARIS (F), 1727—1732, *décharge, minor items*

1790  CALAIS (F), 1768—1774

1791  MANTUA (I), 17th century

1792  VENICE (I), control mark prior to 1810

1793  MILAN (I), control mark prior to 1810

1794  ITALY, 1810—1872, *purity 800/1000, for small items*

1795  VASTERVIK (S), 18th—19th centuries

1796 

HELSINGØR (DK), 1741

1797  STRÖMSTAD (S), 19th century

1798		CORK (Corcaigh) (EIR), 17th—18th centuries; *more variations*
1799		VÄNERSBORG (S), 18th—19th centuries
1800		KOSTROMA (Russia), 1769—1813
1801		VASTERVIK (S), 18th—19th centuries
1802		HJO (S), 18th—19th centuries
1803		KRISTINEHAMN (S), 18th—19th centuries
1804		KOSTROMA (Russia), 1880—1890; *numeral indicates purity*
1805		ITALY, 1810—1872, *purity 950/1000, for large items*
1806		SÖDERHAMN (S), 18th—19th centuries
1807		HELSINKI (SF), up to 1943
1808		CAEN (F), 1744—1750, *décharge, large items*

1809 

BIRMINGHAM (GB), from 1773 to 20th century; *several variations*

1810 

DÜSSELDORF (D), 17th—18th centuries

1811 

NORRTÄLJE (S), 18th—19th centuries

1812 

FORMER CZECHOSLOVAKIA, 1921—1940, *export items*

1813 

ODESSA (Ukraine), 1848

1814 

ST PETERSBURG (Russia), 1851

1815 

ST PETERSBURG (Russia), 1776—1825

1816 

ST PETERSBURG (Russia), last quarter of 19th century; *numeral indicates purity*

EMBLEMS

1817 

KOSTROMA (Russia), 1813—1831

1818 

OPORTO (P), 1911—1938, *silver rods*

1819  GONDOMAR (P), 1913—1938, *silver rods*

1820  ROTTERDAM (NL), 18th century

1821  SPAIN, 1881—1934, *purity 916/1000*

1822  LIÈGE (Luik) (B), 1724—1743

1823  LISBON (P), 1886—1938, *silver rods*

1824  KUTNÁ HORA (CZ), 17th—18th centuries

1825  NOVOCHERKASK (Russia), 1847—1880

1826  GALICIA (Ukraine), 1758—1780

1827  TARTU (Derpt) (Estonia), 1862

1828  TULA (Russia), 1796—19th century

1829  CHESTER (GB), 17th century and from 1780 up to the present; *several variations*

1830  FRIBOURG (CH), mid-18th century

1831 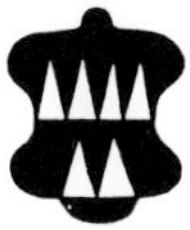 KROMĚŘÍŽ (CZ), up to 1798

1832  SWITZERLAND, "Poinçon de Notoriété"; *imitation of French 18th-century marks*

1833  TONGEREN (Tongres) (B), c. 1759

1834  PARIS (F), 1756—1762, *charge, minor items*

1835  LIÈGE (Luik) (B), 1688—1693

1836  LIÈGE (Luik) (B), 1650—1688

1837  LIÈGE (Luik) (B), 1693—1705?

1838  LIÈGE (Luik) (B), 1711—1723

1839		LIÈGE (Luik) (B), 1744—1763
1840		DENDERMONDE (Termonde) (B), 18th century
1841		LEUVEN (Louvain) (B), 18th century
1842		MÜNSTER in Westfalen (D), 16th—17th centuries; *changing shields*
1843		ZUG (CH), 18th century
1844		ZOFINGEN (CH), 18th century
1845		BRNO (CZ), from mid-16th century to mid-17th century
1846		LAUSANNE (CH), 18th century
1847		KALUGA (Russia), end of 18th century and early 19th century
1848		ZUG (CH), 16th—17th centuries

1849		ULM (D), 17th century
1850		ULM (D), 18th century
1851		ULM (D), 17th—18th centuries
1852		INNSBRUCK (A), 1766—1806
1853		KASSEL (D), 18th century
1854		COLOGNE (D), 2nd half of 17th century; *changing letter*
1855		LIÈGE (Luik) (B), 1772—1784
1856		BADEN in Aargau (CH), 16th—17th centuries
1857		BREGENZ (A), c. 1732
1858		PAYERNE (CH), 16th—17th centuries

1859  **LUCERNE (CH), 16th century**

1860  SWITZERLAND, 17th—18th centuries, *mark for the Lucerne canton*

1861  LUCERNE (CH), 2nd half of 19th century

1862  PFORZHEIM (D), 18th—19th centuries

1863  CHESTER (GB), 1701—1779

1864  HALBERSTADT (D), 18th century; *changing shield*

1865  ANSBACH (D), 17th—18th centuries

1866  BADEN-BADEN (D), 18th—19th centuries

1867  ANSBACH (D), 18th century

1868  KARLSRUHE (D), after 1806

1869		SALINS (F), mid-18th century
1870		UTRECHT (NL), 18th century
1871		ALTENBURG (D), 17th—18th centuries; *not certain whether Altenburg, perhaps Annaberg (D)*
1872		KASSEL (D), 18th—19th centuries; *changing date letter*
1873		NEUCHÂTEL (CH), 1820—1866
1874		HANAU (D), 18th century
1875		HANAU (D), mid-18th century, (Neu-Hanau)
1876		COURTRAI (Kortrijk) (B), from mid-17th century to the end of 18th century
1877		FRANKENTHAL (D), 17th century
1878		WÜRZBURG (D), early 19th century

1879  VIENNA (A) 1790—1866, *for swordmakers' and watchmakers' wares; 13 lot silver only*

1880  VIENNA (A), 1764—1806, *for swordmakers' and watchmakers' wares; 13 lot silver only*

1881  BANSKÁ BYSTRICA (SK), 18th century; *changing date*

1882  BANSKÁ BYSTRICA (SK), 1st half of 19th century; *changing date*

1883  KOŠICE (SK), from c. 1812 to c. 1867; *changing date*

1884  GYÖR (H), from c. 1815 to c. 1860; *changing date*

1885  VIENNA (A), 1691—1737, *changing date; for 13 lot silver*

1886  LINZ (A), 1737(1787?) — 1806; *changing date*

1887  TURIN (I), since 1678; *changing letters in the mark*

1888  ZWOLLE (NL), 18th century

1889 

VIENNA (A), prior to 1530

1890 

VIENNA (A), 1530—1548

1891 

VIENNA (A), 1570—1674

1892 

VIENNA (A), 1675—1737; *changing date*

1893 

VIENNA (A), 1737—1784, *for 15 lot silver; changing date*

1894 

VIENNA (A), 1737—1784, *for 13 lot silver; changing date*

1895 

VIENNA (A), 1791—1806, *for 15 lot silver; changing date*

1896 

VIENNA (A), 1784—1806, *for 13 lot silver; changing date*

1897
1898  

FORMER AUSTRO-HUNGARIAN EMPIRE, 1806—1866, *for 15 lot silver; changing date; for significance of letters in the marks see marks Nos. 1901—1902*

1899
1900

FORMER AUSTRO-HUNGARIAN EMPIRE, 1806—1824, *for 13 lot silver; changing date; for significance of letters in the marks see marks Nos. 1901—1902*

1901
1902

FORMER AUSTRO-HUNGARIAN EMPIRE, 1825—1866, *for 13 lot silver; changing date*

Key to the Marks:
A — Vienna (A)
B — Prague (CZ)
C — Salzburg (A)
D — Lvov (Ukraine)
E — Cracow (PL) only during the 1807—1809 period;
E — Hall (A), 1824—1866
F — Brno (CZ)
G — Linz (A)
H — Graz (A)
I — Klagenfurt (A)
K — Ljubljana (Slovenia)
L — Trieste (I)

1903

CRAILSHEIM (D), 17th century

1904

TÜBINGEN (D), 16th—17th centuries

1905

MONS (Bergen), (B), 18th century

1906

HÄLSINGBORG (S), 19th century

1907

SWITZERLAND, "Poinçon de de Notoriété"; *imitation of French 18th-century marks*

1908

BRZEG (Brieg) (PL), 16th—17th centuries

1909  TOULOUSE (F), 17th century, *charge?*

1910  KROMĚŘÍŽ (CZ), 1769—1806: *changing date*

1911  WSCHOWA (Fraustadt) (PL), 17th—18th centuries

1912  SENLIS (F), 1768—1774, *charge, medium-sized items*

1913  MANTES (F), 1784—1789

1914  STRALSUND (D),17th century

1915  KURSK (Russia), 19th century

1916  U.S.A., Michael Wilcox, 1772—1799, Maryland

1917  BRAY-SUR-SEINE (F), 1768—1774

1918  TOULOUSE (F), 16th—17th centuries, *décharge*

1939  KÖPING (S), c. 1800

1940  KOSTROMA (Russia), 1870s; *numeral indicates purity*

1941  CHERSON (Ukraine), last quarter of 19th century; *numeral indicates purity*

1942  SCHWYZ (CH), 17th—18th centuries

1943  ALOST (Aalst) (B), mid-18th century

1944  BADEN in Aargau (CH), 17th—18th centuries

1945  LAVAL (F), 1728

1946  KALININGRAD (Königsberg) (Russia), late 17th century up to 1800; *more variations*

1947  TURIN (I), 18th century

1948 

KOSTROMA (Russia), 1746

1949		KONSTANZ (D), 19th century
1950		ELBLĄG (Elbing) (PL), late 17th century and 18th century
1951		GDAŃSK (Danzig) (PL), 17th—18th centuries
1952		BREDA (NL), 17th century
1953		AMSTERDAM (NL), 18th century
1954		HAMMELBURG (D), early 18th century
1955		PADERBORN (D), 17th century
1956		TÜBINGEN (D), 18th century
1957		TBILISI (Tiflis) (Georgia), last quarter of 19th century

1958		DEBRECEN (H), 2nd half of 18th century
1959		LEVOČA (SK), from 16th to early 19th century; *shield changes shape*
1960		IEPER (Ypres) (B), 2nd half of 17th century
1961		KONSTANZ (D), 18th century
1962		KONSTANZ (D), late 17th century
1963		LEVOČA (SK), 1st half of 19th century
1964		FORMER CZECHOSLOVAKIA, 1929—1940, *purity 950/1000*
1965		FORMER CZECHOSLOVAKIA, 1929—1940, *purity 925/1000*
1966		FORMER CZECHOSLOVAKIA, 1929—1940, *purity 900/1000*
1967		FORMER CZECHOSLOVAKIA, 1929—1940, *purity 835/1000*
1968		FORMER CZECHOSLOVAKIA, 1929—1940, *purity 800/1000*

1969  TURKEY, 1923, *purity 900/1000*

1970  TURKEY, 1923, *purity 800/1000*

1971  TUNISIA, 1856—1905, *"Khálés" confirmation*

1972  TUNISIA, 1856—1905, *"Sahha" guarantee*

1973  TUNISIA, 1856—1905, *"Sekka" purity (900/1000)*

1974  TUNIS (TN), 1856—1905, *beys' marks*

1975  TUNIS (TN), 1856—1905, *beys' marks*

1976  TUNIS (TN), 1856—1905, *beys' marks*

1977  TUNIS (TN), 1856—1905, *beys' marks*

1978  DJERBA (TN), 1856—1905

1979

SOUSSE (TN), 1856—1905

1980

SFAX (TN), 1856—1905

1981

GABES (TN), 1856—1905

1982

TURKEY, 1844—1923, *purity 900/1000*

1983
1984
1985

BENI SUEF (ET), since 1916, *purity 900/1000; 800/1000; 600/1000*

1986
1987
1988

TANTA (ET), since 1916, *purity 900/1000; 800/1000; 600/1000*

1989
1990
1991

CAIRO (ET), since 1916, *purity 900/1000; 800/1000; 600/1000*

1992
1993
1994

ALEXANDRIA (ET), since 1916, *purity 900/1000; 800/1000; 600/1000*

INDEX OF CITIES AND COUNTRIES

INDEX OF AMERICAN MASTERS